Why Christianity Fails In America

Sequel to the American Church Growth Classic
Why Churches Die

"...To make Christianity viable in the
Twenty-first Century, there must be
an internal redirection of the
Protestant spirit."

Hollis L. Green, ThD, PhD

GlobalEdAdvancePress
37321-7635 USA

This book is dedicated to a Congregation
that has demonstrated for the past decade
that Christianity can work
in an American community:
New Life Baptist Church
Bluff City, Tennessee.

Copyright © 2007

Global Educational Advance Inc.
Tennessee 37321-7635

Printed in the United States of America

Published by

GlobalEdAdvancePress
http://www.GlobalEdAdvance.org
ISBN 978-0-9796019-1-0

CONTENTS

A distinguished professor of education and social change, Hollis L. Green, ThD, PhD, has taught at the graduate level for three decades. A Diplomate in the Oxford Society of Scholars, he has authored 26 books and numerous articles, served pastorates in five states, and lectured in over 100 countries.

Dr. Green was the founding President (1981) and Chancellor (1991) of Oxford Graduate School, U.S.A. and founded Oasis University (2002) in Trinidad, W.I. In 2007 he launched Global Educational Advance, Inc. Dr. Green's books are a logical outgrowth of his ministry through education.

PROLOGUE

Christianity Can Work in America

Despite dire predictions, Christianity is alive and well. Friedrich Nietzsche's 1882 calculation about the early decline in religious faith was wrong. At the turn of the last century, George Bernard Shaw and H. G. Wells both predicted an end to what they called the religious phase of history. Even as late as mid-century Julian Huxley wrote about God's last fading smile and compared it to the grin of a Cheshire cat. None of these secular prophets were correct. God was not dead. Christianity did not fade away as an old soldier.

A structured program may not work, but the personal witness utilized in life-style evangelism will bring great dividends. It may take faith, fire, and fumigation to create an atmosphere conducive to renewal, but individual participation is the answer. As believers walk in faith and demonstrate the love of Christ, renewal and revival will come.

Notwithstanding the difficulties that exist in ministering in a pluralistic society, Christians should be optimistic that the prayers for revival will be answered. Christians must reach out beyond the stained-glass barrier and take the message of saving grace to the community. This is not the time to wait in the church sanctuary for some program to work. Unbelievers will not stumble into the worship service seeking salvation. The witness of God's love and mercy must be taken to the streets, shared in the byways, and proclaimed in the market place. When this is achieved by sincere believers who demonstrate love and understanding, converts will be made and the church will triumph.

Although the appeal of organized sectarian religion has declined, America's general faith in God and interest in religion has grown during the last century. The faith fostered by First-century Christians is still flourishing in many parts of the world. Christianity has made recent surges in Africa, revival has returned to China, and the church has made a substantial comeback in Russia. The Twenty-first Century could be the greatest time for Christianity. The Bible predicted that in the "last days" God would pour out His Spirit upon all flesh. In the midst of a decaying society, Christians can hope for renewal and revival. When Christ returns, there will be faith on the earth! This I firmly believe!

Focus of the Book

The only hope for a viable Christianity is an internal redirection of the soul that brings with it a personal commitment to the cardinal tenets of the Christian Faith and a spirit of cooperation and trust. In addition to the problems of "name brand Christianity" and "freeze frame theology", One Lord, One Faith and One Baptism have become 300-plus CHURCHES with antagonistic leaders, competing agendas, and opposing methodologies. Leaders must take the initiative to bring renewal and restoration to local congregations and make evangelism and missions central to the local programming.

Is the progressive decline of Christianity in America inevitable? Is the character and social fabric of a pluralistic society so complicated that Christianity cannot work in America? Evidence exists that Christianity could work if small changes were made in both the attitude and action of professing Christians. In isolated areas, individual Christians are practicing their faith effectively and some local congregations are alive and growing. Sadly, this is not true of the total Movement in America. For the most part, congregations seem to be fragmented, stagnant, and unable to communicate a unified message to the public.

Why does Christianity fail in a given culture? What is the inferior operation that weakens the witness? The Christian message ceases to be a viable expression of faith when congregations: .

——fail to associate with local culture
——fail to accentuate commonalties
——fail to advance a melting pot
——fail to attest personal behavior
——fail to augment the value of families
——fail to advocate relational theology
——fail to avow Christian culture
——fail to affirm people
——fail to amplify quality
——fail to assure substance
——fail to accent heritage
——fail to adopt principles

The blueprint for constructing an effective local congregation is to take a positive stand and strive to move forward in all the areas where the congregation now fails to measure up to all aspects of the Great Commission. Until the areas of difficulty are understood, a superior congregation will not develop. The diagnosed failures must be corrected before a plan of action can be executed.

Clyde Reid (1967), in his work on preaching and communication, declared the American pulpit to be empty. In the intervening decades, the empty pulpit syndrome has produced half-filled churches and half-hearted commitment to the basic tenets of the Christian Faith.   Any defense of the viability of Christianity in America today is to suggest that the structures of the past are good enough for today and the future.   This is certainly not true in any other aspect of life or history. The church is made up of people, and people change.   The church exists in a society, and societies change.   Change is the one constant factor of modern life. The structure, message, and communication of American Christianity must change to maintain any semblance of viability in the future.

In the first decade of the Twenty-first Century, the situation is even worse. Congregations have been unable to bridge the great fixed gulf between church and state or to reduce the negative effect of an intrusive government into the life-style of church members. Although American Presidents have identified with Christianity and related to a specific denomination, the "pulpit" of the Presidency together with the combined pulpits of thousands of churches were unable to stem the tide of moral decay and progressive debauchery in American life. Clergy involvement in public life and political causes has not prevented discrimination or eliminated injustice in American society.

Drastic changes are required in American Christianity for the "communications super-highway" and other certain cultural and technological innovations in the fast paced Twenty-first Century. In America, a cultural framework for doctrine has created a brand name concept for local congregations. This development was based on century-old writings of past theologians and produced a freeze frame theology not relevant to the present generation.

Many congregations have failed to transmit adequate experiential knowledge of the Christian life to succeeding generations to make genuine converts. This, coupled with the mobility of society, produced complex and confusing relationships within local congregations. Consequently, many unintentionally hinder the conversion and disciplined life-style of the next generation. To make Christianity viable in the Twenty-first Century, there must be an internal redirection of the soul that includes a return to a personal Christian experience, commitment, and accountability.

Rationale for the Book

My half-century attempt to support Christianity at the congregational level required a generic blindness to the sectarian nature of American CHURCHES and provided a less biased framework for social research related to American Christianity. The effort to understand the church as a social institution and develop an appreciation for my religious heritage enhanced my personal Christian life and provided a basis for continued research.   My search for antecedent causes for cultural divisions has taken me into every region of the United States and required extensive travel in many countries.

Research was directed toward the social and cultural foundations of American CHURCHES. The problem of negative participation in the worship and programming of local congregations created a declining attendance, as well as the destructive aspects of personal mental reservation to commitment and cognitive dissent to doctrine.   In an effort to understand some sectarian views, extensive research was done on the oldest American Pentecostal denomination and the largest American Protestant group. Doctorates in Theology and Philosophy were earned during this search. Meanwhile, my schedule has been filled with academic administration, research and writing, but colleagues and friends have encouraged another book as a sequel to my best known work, Why Churches Die.

Over the years, this research has been reported in various books: Dynamics of Christian Discipleship dealt with the individual and personal nature of the Christian life. Marching As To War was a denominational history. Understanding Pentecostalism was an effort to grasp the effect of church doctrine on individual members and understand what was happening on the American scene. Why Churches Die presented the difficulties of operating the church as a social institution or business organization without spiritual foundation.   Why Wait Till Sunday suggested a plan for renewal of a weak congregation troubled by the "human factor" and the problem of "upward delegation." Understanding Scientific Research was a research text for the social professions in an effort to get others involved in research related to morality and ethics in business and industry, principles and values in the social professions, and the sociological integration of religion into American society. Why Christianity Fails in America is a logical sequel to some of my previous works.

CHAPTER BY CHAPTER REVIEW

Chapter One:

CONGREGATIONS FAIL TO ASSOCIATE WITH LOCAL CULTURE

Most congregations are more interested in their doctrine and polity than connecting with the local community. Organized religion fails to join the interest or purpose of the people of a particular locale. Always some higher, more pressing agenda imposes both method and message on the people rather than meeting the needs of the community. Local congregations seem to have no partnership, no walking together or joining forces to meet the goals of the common people. Congregations require the people to adapt to the program of the church, whether it meets their needs or not. Congregations often identify with dogma rather than location and in doing so violate the basic principles of communicating a common gospel.

Chapter Two:

CONGREGATIONS FAIL TO ACCENTUATE COMMONALTIES

Churches emphasize differences rather than sameness or commonalties. A cultural framework for doctrine has created a brand name concept for American churches based on distinctive teachings of the past. Little effort is made to accentuate the common ground that exists for all Christian groups. This failure heightens the effect of the differences rather than the commonalties. The emphasis on difference divides the message into so many parts that the public cannot construct the whole. Much of the meaning is lost in the diverse and segmented message.

Only through commonalties can knowledge be advanced, yet congregations constantly emphasize their differences. This dissimilarity in Christian groups is a tragic flaw that divides the whole into vulnerable and indefinable parts and presents a misleading message. Sadly, this is done as if the process of stating distinctive differences were an asset. In reality, it is a drawback to the public understanding of the Christian Faith and a liability to individual and institutional cooperation in areas where there should be a common agenda and message that could easily facilitate a melting pot for all cultures and ethnic groups.

Chapter Three:

CONGREGATIONS FAIL TO ADVANCE A MELTING POT

Churches produce a stew pot rather than a melting pot. The ethnic and culturally based denominational structure of Protestantism contributes to the American stew pot. Trying to be all things to all men, the church fails to demonstrate the basic idea that the good news of the gospel is for everyone. The little kingdoms, established to protect a particular cultural expression of religion, send the wrong message to the masses. A failure to agree on doctrine and polity contributes to the mixed message and creates an attitude of exclusivity for most congregations. The unintended message is one of exclusion. The true intent of inclusion is lost in the subliminal message of the architecture, the program, and the personal behavior of the local congregation. People are tired of words; the public seems to say to the church "show me!"

Chapter Four:

CONGREGATIONS FAIL TO ATTEST PERSONAL BEHAVIOR

The church fails to bear witness to the Christian behavior appropriate for those who claim membership. There is no effort to certify moral and ethical behavior as a model; in fact, the behavior of many church-related folk suggests that the opposite is acceptable. Positive role models are absent, and little effort is made to support those who rise above the standards of society. The public receives more data on "heroes" and "champions" from the secular press and the sports arena than from the church. Churches promote activities that do not value families.

Chapter Five:

CONGREGATIONS FAIL TO AUGMENT THE VALUE OF FAMILIES

Churches embrace family values rather than the value of families. The church has failed to adequately influence American families. Church and family life have become part of the American stew pot. Parents are one reason the present generation has turned off the mixed message of the church. A hypocritical lifestyle, blatant immorality, and the obvious unhappiness, all express the failure of the family unit. Since families are the building blocks of the church, the family is a reflection of the church itself. When controversy and friction are present in the home, it complicates the function of the local church and the general witness of Christianity.

The dysfunctional nature of families within the church is about the same as those in the general public. Although this may speak to the deterioration of American society, the church must accept some responsibility for the failure of the family under their care. Does the church not have an obligation to persuade families in the direction they ought to go? Is this not the essence of Christianity? The church has been aggressively hypocritical in insisting on family values but not modeling or teaching the value of families.

A lack of role models and accountability for failure clearly exists. To make churches viable in the Twenty-first Century, there must be an internal redirection of the Protestant spirit with less emphasis on sectarianism and parochial adherence to particular CHURCHES, and more emphasis on the value of families. To adequately teach the value of families, the church must have both a family friendly program and a relational theology.

Chapter Six:

CONGREGATIONS FAIL TO ADVOCATE RELATIONAL THEOLOGY

Christianity has not established a relational theology for the congregation. The Christian community has made little effort for a more practical approach to the reality of theological interpretation. Generally, an application of theology to behavior has been neglected. The concept of the Incarnation should prompt theologians to make some linkage between theology and human behavior, but the persistent effort has been to organize theology based on the thoughts and "opinions" of other generations with little contemporary application. Most congregations reproduce an intellectual and systematic theology rather than relational theology appropriate to the development of a Christian culture. Doing this they fail to support a Christian culture that supplants the evil within the general and specific culture.

Chapter Seven:

CONGREGATIONS FAIL TO AVOW CHRISTIAN CULTURE

Christianity did not begin within a single culture or ethnic group, but brought people together into a common life from a wide diversity of races, cultures and backgrounds. Early churches started in houses and involved whole families. Early Christianity developed the elements of a common culture that served as an umbrella simultaneously for most subcultures. When individuals accepted Christianity, some of their lifestyle and practices changed, but not all. The converts remained and functioned within their native culture, but identified with the larger Christian community.

Christianity, as an organized religion expressed in the local churches today, owes much in its history to many others than its professional elite. Many made significant contributions to the cause: scholars, writers, artists, architects, and historians; scientists, philosophers with ideas, and men of action; yes, even converts from the shady side of life.   The professional leadership was shaped both by their culture and by the nature of Christianity.   In spite of this, local congregations today develop civil rather than Christian culture and fail to affirm people in the context of their local culture and community.   The church must affirm people to advance the cause of Christianity.

Chapter Eight:

CONGREGATIONS FAIL TO AFFIRM PEOPLE

Sameness in buildings has replaced the common aspects of faith.   Churches build buildings rather than concentrating on structuring the lives of people. Buildings have become the most static part of organized religion, especially in a society characterized by mobility. The large investment of funds in single use property has become the greatest detriment to the general progress of Christianity. Deserted church buildings point to a former presence and the departure of a constituency.   These buildings send a message of paradise lost and breed contempt for the Christian faith.   An abandoned church building sends a message that Christianity is not relevant to the community.

Churches should stay and minister to the community and go and grow by planting churches elsewhere. It is never profitable to abandon a community where God has placed a church. What about the people left behind? The message of faith must be established in people, not property. The objective ought to be confidently assisting individuals in establishing positive structures for relationships, but the effort to construct buildings continues.   In an effort to increase attendance, the church relocates before the local people have been reached. Did God not guide and provide funds to build the building in a given community? Is it wise to abandon a community before the task is completed? Quantity is often more important than quality.

Chapter Nine:
CONGREGATIONS FAIL TO AMPLIFY QUALITY

Local congregations seek quantity rather than quality. A Christian congregation should be both adequate and effective.   Quality and quantity are mutually exclusive; increasing one will decrease the other.   There must be proportional balance between these two elements to maintain a viable state in any organization. The dynamic aspects of organizational growth and development go through predictable stages. A failure to understand these phases locks the thinking of a congregation into attitudes that handicap the effectiveness of communicating to the community.   When congregations emphasize structure and buildings, the real meaning of reaching the people and propagating the Christian Faith is lost.

Chapter Ten:
CONGREGATIONS FAIL TO ASSURE SUBSTANCE

Churches advance structure rather than substance. The message of organized religion is always confused by the past. The facts of each story clearly point to a reality of living with, living down or living up to the past. This so complicates the present message as to make it void of current value to many people. The extreme variability on the one hand and a basic similarity on the other prompt various expressions as to the viability of the local church.

Religion clearly has a future, but a conclusive statement regarding the future of the local church in a pluralistic society cannot be predicted from the existing data. There is too much controversial evidence, too many different opinions to make a conclusive statement about the future of Christianity in American society. Only God can see the future. The work of God will not fail.

Individual churches, local congregations may fail to reach their communities for Christ, but the message of Grace will be propagated. It will not come by the personality of a television preacher or the program of the institutional church, but by the Spirit of God working though believing individuals who are committed to share their faith with family, friends, and in the market place. The legacy of personal witness in the context of ones personal community and heritage is a powerful tool for outreach and is in keeping with the basic expansion of the gospel.

Chapter Eleven:

CONGREGATIONS FAIL TO ADOPT PRINCIPLES

Leaders in Christianity should embrace the principles and claims of a common faith as their own. It is a matter of choice, but often the choice is not made to follow the principles by either the leadership or the members of local congregations. Many local churches fail to accept the generalization that scripture has authenticity, and fail to use the essence of the faith as a basis for reason or conduct. Religious leaders should remember that a failed philosophy of Communism was "The end justifies the means." Just because a process or procedure works for the moment does not mean that it is good for the ongoing program of the local church.

Notwithstanding, local congregations continue to embrace pragmatism rather than principle and in doing so fail to communicate basic principles of Christianity.

Chapter Twelve:

CONGREGATIONS FAIL TO ACCENT HERITAGE

Practices handed down from the past by tradition become customary behavior normally respected by the next generation. The church must respect these traditions and work within the framework of one's heritage in presenting the gospel. God does not require anyone to move outside their culture and language to hear the gospel. Christianity has been an effective instrument in social change in some aspects of society, but the church has all but ignored many aspects of heritage and imposed programs that are counter productive; local churches often sanction political correctness rather than heritage. Family, race, and ethnicity are valuable aspects of heritage. The church suffers when these aspects of heritage are neglected.

I. CONGREGATIONS FAIL TO ASSOCIATE WITH LOCAL CULTURE

Churches identify with dogma rather than location.

Most congregations are more interested in their doctrine and polity than connecting with the local community. Organized religion fails to join the interest or purpose of the people of a particular locale. Always some higher, more pressing agenda imposes both method and message on the people rather than meeting the needs of the community. Local congregations seem to have no partnership, no walking together or joining forces to meet the goals of the people. Protestant congregations require the people to adapt to the program of the church, whether it meets community needs or not.

In the New Testament and throughout church history, Christian congregations were identified with the culture and the people of a particular location. Each local gathering of believers was perceived as a part of the universal church whether in Jerusalem, Antioch, Corinth, Ephesus, or in Asia. Each house church was recognized and presented in Scripture as people of a particular village, town, or region of a country. Collectively, the congregations made up the church in a particular place and were considered to be part of the universal church. This suggested a sameness or cultural similarity within a congregation, a kind of broad-based homogeneity that does not exist in the pluralistic society of today.   This obvious diversity or difference is a basic difficulty for local congregations. Religious organizations that reach coast to coast and border to border cannot achieve sameness. Rather than distinguish the various subcultures and work within the indigenous culture, CHURCHES seem to strive for universal sameness as an identity.   The sameness should relate to the common ground in the Christian Faith rather than the specific sectarian differences of a denomination.

It has become a kind of ecclesiastical franchise with institutional inspectors to assure conformity to the protocols of sameness.   A certain code of conduct, a particular form of religious ceremony, and specific ecclesiastical etiquette must be observed to be a bona fide member of the franchise.   The process has imposed cultural barriers on people when only one thing separated man from God, his disbelief and disobedience.   Yet, variations in culture and custom can alienate one from the local church and a church from a denomination.   Whether it is music, food, clothing, or general atmosphere, if it is not in keeping with ones basic culture, the local church becomes less attractive.   When, in the Name of Christ, one is forced to perform or conform within an alien culture, there is little hope that the gospel will take root and grow within a culture or particular subculture.

In First-century Christianity, no one gave up ethnic heritage or cultural identity to become a Christian   believer;   in fact, converts were never required to cross cultural or linguistic barriers to receive the basic witness of the Christian Faith. The Christian message was taken to their home area and presented in the native language within the limitations of their culture. A Jew did not give up the Jewish heritage with a decision to follow Jesus Christ. A Gentile was not required to first become a Jew to embrace the Christian Faith. Perhaps God never intended to force cultural change on individuals; no wonder such attempts fail. Remember the early Council of the Church in Jerusalem dealing with pagan converts:

For it seemed good to the Holy Ghost, and to us, to lay upon you no greater burden than these necessary things; that ye abstain from meat offered to idols, and from blood, and from things strangled, and from fornication: from which if ye keep yourselves, ye shall do well. (Acts 15:28, 29)

One great battle in the leadership of the Apostle Paul was to protect the Gentile converts from the encroachment of Jewish customs and practices. Although they remained Jewish or Gentile in culture and many practices remained the same, converts became something more than their culture; however, they continued to function adequately within their native culture, even within their professions. Converts became a part of a larger family. It was a new birth, a new beginning. They were a part of a new and growing culture that they later identified as Christian. The objective was to superimpose a larger cultural framework on society, within which all individuals could function with minimum changes to their basic culture. Christianity was to separate converts from their "sins" not from their friends and family.

Although it appears that Christian congregations of the First-century were homogeneous, this was not by design. It happened because of the customs and civilization of some particular people with the limitation of communication and travels. Although this produced a particular cultural brand of Christianity, a larger, more comprehensive, even an all-consuming Christian culture emerged throughout the known world. The experience transformed their character. As individual believers accepted the basic proposition of the Christian Faith, there was a personal transformation into a "new creation." In fact, the Christian experience enhanced their established lifestyle. For example, the soldiers who converted to Christianity were told to remain in the military, but to permit Christian principles to guide them in not abusing their authority.

At times, miraculous intervention brought the good news to both individuals and groups. Occasionally, First-century Jews from many nations gathered for the Jerusalem Feast of Pentecost. The time had come for the rapid expansion of Christianity; consequently, God intervened. There was no time for extensive language training or preparation for missionary evangelism. In Jerusalem, individuals from various nations and languages received the witness of God's grace in their native tongue. The experience at the Feast of Pentecost was primarily one of evangelism. The lesson was that God intended every nation to hear the gospel in their native culture and tongue. Did the church not learn the true lesson of Pentecost? The pluralistic society of America seems similar to the multifaceted culture that existed in First-century Jerusalem. Instead of waiting for a divine encounter, churches attempt to manipulate the people and the culture; consequently, the effort ends in relative failure.

The history and dogma of a particular religious group in America are also tied to the persecutions and problems within the historical context of the originating country. Wars, the famines, the ruling class, the form of government, religious persecution, even the socioeconomic condition, all made impact on the cultural view of a particular brand of religious expression. Gradually they gave a brand name and promoted these particular interpretations of religious doctrines as the proper, best, or only way to present the gospel. It may have been the best for a particular subculture, but to propagate a specific approach to all cultures nationally or internationally would be a different story altogether.

A cultural framework for establishing doctrinal positions has been the norm in American Protestantism. Some American groups developed congregations out of the historical and cultural conditions of the American scene. Congregations of the Restoration Movement and such groups as the Holiness and Pentecostal Movement are examples. It seems that cultural foundations can identify most, if not all, American denominational groups. These cultural and regional origins have colored various interpretations of Scripture. Over time these various interpretations of religious teachings were given brand names and promoted as the correct or proper way to present the gospel.

Most Christian groups and Protestant CHURCHES can be traced to cultural roots or national origins. The Roman Catholic identity is obvious. The Church of England, the Greek and Russian Orthodox Churches have obvious national origins. Methodist and Episcopal congregations have English origins, Presbyterians have Scottish roots,

Lutherans have foundations in Germany, Baptists have European beginnings, and the list goes on. At one time in America, among the many Baptist groups, there was a Swedish Baptist Church. When this particular denomination stopped growing they were told, "You have run out of Swedes." The name was changed to provide broader appeal and the group continued to grow. American Christianity has created congregations clustered around theological constructs which brand names have identified and advanced as an accurate interpretation of scripture.

The Bible, which was supposed to be the Word of God for all people, has been viewed through cultural glasses and the private interpretation differs from group to group. Consequently, universal truth became the exclusive domain of a particular religious authority and limited to a selected doctrinal or denominational constituency. Various teachings and different doctrine were culturally interpreted but firmly proclaimed authoritatively as the true and proper expression of the Bible. While Judaism, Roman Catholics, and members of Islam have differences, a unified message is presented to the world. Protestant churches accentuate their differences as a badge of honor. Each group behaving as if they have found the Holy Grail and have exclusive access to the secrets of Christianity or the keys to heaven.

American Judaism has small internal differences, but the Jewish community maintains a unified identity.   When individuals are identified as being Jewish, one immediately has an idea of their basic values. Judaism has a sense of community and commitment to the individual and family. The public understands the sameness of the essential elements of Jewish worship and commitments.

Although some differences exist among Roman Catholics, they manage to present a unified voice to the average American citizen.   Others, whether Mormons, Jehovah's Witnesses, or Islam, manage to overcome differences and present a common identity. This is not true of Protestant Christianity, greatly complicating the advance of basic Christian teachings.

American Protestants are not identified as "Christian," but as Baptist, Methodist, Lutheran, Pentecostal, and the list goes on and on. As if this were not enough division, multiple identities and doctrines exist within each of these groups. Is this a result of the pluralism in America, inevitable for an immigrant nation?   Can American Christians not lay aside small doctrinal differences and develop a unified identity around common tenets?   Are there no converts to the Christian Faith, just believers in sectarian dogma? Must each individual who embraces the Christian Faith be branded and identified as free-range cattle belonging to a particular ranch or rancher?

Authority is a major aspect of religion. All religious groups have either some inspired text, a sacred authority figure, an ecclesiastical tribunal, or some combination of these that is considered to be indisputable and final in matters of faith and practice. The unquestioned acceptance of this authority in each group causes the views of others to be less authentic or invalid. This brand name dogma, put forth by an authority and generally accepted as true without question by the followers of that authority, has produced a mixed message and prevented a united voice for Christianity in America. How can one expect the religious folk of America to follow the Christian Church into battle, when the gospel trumpet comes from so many uncertain directions?   Whom shall the people follow? Without clear direction, they follow no one.

Since early Christian congregations were homogeneous to the culture in which they were located, one would logically assume that this would be a natural phenomenon of a Christian church. It would be expected that a local church would reflect the community in which it is located. This would be true if there were one church made up of all believers in the community as it was in the First-century, but now in America there is name brand advertising and shopping for a church. There are always culturally specific statements to attract certain groups. Others need not appear or apply.

Relocation in the mobile society causes a family to shop for a church identified by a doctrine, not by location.   If one has a Methodist background, the local Baptist church may be passed by although it is more conveniently located.   A Lutheran may live next door to an Episcopal Church, but travel several miles to a church, which matches the dogma previously, taught.   In other words, members of Protestant churches are conscious of brand named institutions identified by the culture, customs, and dogma commonly held by a historic group.   This may be because of national and ethnic animosity or it may be an inevitable consequence of the American culture.   Regardless of the cause, it weakens the voice and divides the effectiveness of American Christianity.

When Barnabas became the leader of the church in Antioch (Acts 11), he soon realized the new believers needed more than he alone could provide.   Barnabas traveled to Tarsus to find Paul and brought him back to Antioch to assist with the instruction and training of converts. This was done in spite of the many differences between Paul of Tarsus and Barnabas from Cyprus.   There were also differences in citizenship, former status in Judaism and even tribal ancestry: Paul was from the tribe of Benjamin and Barnabas from the tribe of Levi.   Yet Paul and Barnabas put aside individual and cultural differences and worked together within the common bond of Christianity to acculturate and assimilate converts into the Christian congregations of Antioch.   For one whole year, Barnabas and Paul taught the disciples at Antioch.   As a result of this combined effort with the Antioch disciples, they were the first believers to be called "Christian."

Could there be some generic system of instruction to follow conversion, which would produce a common identity within the Christian culture? Can converts not simply be disciples of Jesus Christ in their own city and among their own family?   Could believers simply develop a generic Christian life-style and follow Jesus? Must each convert be branded and herded under the teaching of others?   Is there no power or validity in the conversion experience to change individual lives and transform them into the image of Christ? The objective of Christ's great commission was the making of Christian disciples, not branding converts for a particular dogma.

This is not to suggest that America needs a lowest common denominator Christianity. Social and cultural differences will always exist in religious groups. Rather, it points to the simplicity and power of the Christian Faith and the need to emphasize common tenets that bring believers together. The Church is a social institution, and the Christian way of life should be a force to unite rather than divide. The human factor must not be allowed to complicate the universal values of Christianity. Individuals cannot be reached if the message or the methods attempts to extract them from their local culture. Scripture predicted in Isaiah that the "highway of holiness would be so plain that no traveler would err." Believers must find their "place under the sun" and practice their faith in the practical context of their own environment. To make Christianity work each convert must grow beyond sectarian dogma and become parts of the universal Christian movement and be ready, willing and able to practice a personal faith in their own hometown. Brand name religion that segregates believers into cubicles based on dogma will never produce a sufficient number of viable congregations to fulfill Christ's commission. Differences must be minimized and an emphasis placed on commonalties in order to produce cooperation and unity among Christians.

The pluralism of America is put aside at times of national crisis or celebration. During wars and other times of crisis, individuals from all walks of life live and join together to restore peace and tranquility to the lives of their countrymen. After National Elections, for a moment, the political parties lay aside their differences and affect a peaceful transfer of power. Individuals rise above petty differences to the commonalties of citizenship. It would assist the cause of Christianity if Protestant churches would present themselves as a community of faith and accentuate the sharing of basic principles and common Christian attributes.

II. CONGREGATIONS FAIL TO ACCENTUATE COMMONALITIES

Churches emphasize differences rather than commonalties.

A cultural framework for doctrine has created a brand name concept for Christian congregations based on distinctive teachings. Little evidence exists to accentuate the common ground that relates to all Christian groups. This failure heightens the effect of the differences rather than the commonalties. The emphasis on difference divides the message into so many parts that the public cannot construct the whole. Much of the meaning is lost in the diverse and segmented message.

Dissimilarity is a tragic flaw that divides the Christian movement into sectarian units and presents a misleading message. Only through commonalties can one advance basic knowledge, yet local congregations constantly emphasize sectarian differences. Sadly, this is done as if the process of stating distinctive differences were an asset. In reality it is a drawback to public understanding of the Christian Faith and a liability to individual and institutional cooperation in areas where there should be a common agenda.

Confusion exists among Christian groups as to the differences between being distinct and being distinctive. Part of the problem is a lack of understanding of the idea of being distinct. To be distinct is to be dissimilar and clearly seen. On the other hand, to be distinctive is to be one not commonly found elsewhere and suggests exclusivity. The attempt to distinguish one Christian group from another based on distinctive doctrine does not adequately present the group to the public. In fact, it breaks down the quality of the whole group by an emphasis on the lack of a unified message. Emphasizing the differences to distinguish one group from another is to distort the general impression of a common Christian movement.

The public has a right to assume that a Christian group would share the same or similar Christian teachings with other groups that claim to be a part of the same whole. To be whole, no part may be removed or left out. When significant differences in the various groups are evident, the public begins to question the validity of the whole. This creates a public identity crisis for Christianity.

The concept of identity is one of being identical or having sameness; however, differences exist within the individuals or groups which make up the whole. Even identical twins that develop from a single egg have differences. Scholars note identical twins for sameness, not almost indistinguishable differences. The appearance is so similar that only close relatives can recognize the differences.   It should be this way with the Christian movement.   Those who are a part of the inner circle may see the differences and understand their cultural causes, but the public should never have to sort through a jumbled message.   A unified message of common grace and common faith should be projected to the public.

Differences are not consequential enough to change the population of heaven. When groups differ in a particular understanding of a scripture, does that alter the actual meaning?   Both parties could be wrong. Individual understanding of scripture does not change the meaning. Neither will differences in doctrine change the names written in the Lamb's Book of Life.   Different cultural interpretations of particular aspects of scripture may exist, but a central theme and message must be presented. When this common message is distorted by sectarian views, the public is confused.

The denominational paradigm was first constructed to classify the differences academia saw in the various units of Protestant Christianity. The word actually means the act of naming or classifying a unit as to value. Academia saw the results of the sectarian divisions and utilized the concept of "denomination" to demonstrate the different values that each unit placed on particular scriptural teachings. The academics may argue that the concept was religion-neutral and used simply to show differences; however, the word itself is a pejorative construct and is uncomplimentary. The word is defined as an "alias, appellation, code name, epithet, label, or nickname." Most see the word as negative. It should be remembered that one can never reach a positive conclusion beginning with a negative premise.   This paradigm is definitely negative, but Christianity is stuck with the classification.

The same word "denomination" is used to differentiate the value of currency. All the coins and bills are "money" but each has a different value. Is that what is meant in Christianity by "denomination?" All the units are "Christian" but each has a different value?   Denomination is a word imposed on Protestant Christianity by academia trying to express a classification of units as to value. Do some folk belong to a 10-cent church, others to a dollar church, or is everyone searching for the million dollar unit? One can clearly see the confusion that denominationalism brings to the public conception and understanding of Christianity. Satan had a strategy: divide and conquer. Currently, the strategy is working.

Academia classifies the body politic in America as Democrat, Republican, or Independent to illustrate the different understanding of each Party as to democracy and a free-market economy. All these individuals are good Americans who would give their life for the "land of the free and the home of the brave." However, these classifications also identify the deeply divided political party system that has separated the American electorate into bickering groups and created a circumstance where often a minority rules. Half of the eligible voters do not register to vote. Only half of the registered voters actually vote, but half of these cast ballads for the loser. This means that the individual elected is placed in office by a minority of the voters. Is this a good system? To paraphrase a famous quote: "This is the worst system, except for all the others!"

Should not all be a part of the Family of God, the First Family, and the holy and universal church? A family circle is a group that is similar and connected. This association causes a blending of mind and heart. Certainly, a family has differences, but similarities characterize primary groups. One speaks of a family circle when describing close relatives or a family tree when describing how individuals are related.   They have a sameness, which determines the family identity, yet there are surely difference in appearance, personality, and character.

Differences are in the background, as new members are welcomed into the larger family circle.   Whether it is the family photo album or a genealogical chart, it is the sameness, the similarity that identifies the kinship relationship. Has the Christian church lost the concept of family? Is there no sameness?   Must each group present a distinctive message to the world and project a divided movement?

The Family of God on earth deserves a simple and clear message to the world. The fabric of families is made up of divergent strands which come together to make a single unit. Two strands may be twisted together to form yarn for use in creating fabric, but at least three strands are required to braid or plait a strong and useful thread. Two strands alone cannot form a strong union; a third stand is required to provide strength for the unit. In the case of a couple coming together in marriage, this third strand is a sense of family, which permeates the commitment and supplies the adhesive for a strong bond. The wise man Solomon said, "Two are better than one.... and a cord with three strands is not quickly broken." It is this third strand that Solomon must have considered being the strength of the union. The common message of faith and grace must be proclaimed by each part of the Christian movement or the credibility of the whole is in jeopardy.

The same is true of religious groups, when a group attempts to stand alone or limit association with a few who are "just the same," the binding strand which brings strength is missing. There is some value in diversity, but there is vitality in common ground. Groups, which insist on projecting dissimilarity in structure and doctrine, will remain weak without a sense of commitment to commonalties that could inform their participation in the larger community of faith. Sectarian groups that isolate themselves from the whole by emphasizing the distinctive nature of a particular teaching rather than a common identity with the community of faith will suffer limitations and remain earthen vessels without the spiritual dynamic to advance the Christian cause.

There is strength in unity and weakness in division. Jesus was clear in Scripture, "If a house is divided against itself, that house cannot stand." This was said in the context of the reality that Satan would never permit his work to be divided. Perhaps the differences within American Christianity proceed from an evil strategy to "divide and conquer."

Even groups that express certain uniqueness and differentiate themselves from others receive nurture and sustenance from the larger community. Lacking a common identity with the community of faith, such groups do not contribute to the strength of the larger body. The strand, which tethers them to the community of faith, becomes umbilical cords carrying nourishment from the larger unit. In some cases this seems to be a one way street.

Such groups become "takers" without giving a fair share commitment to the infrastructure, which forms the basis for their existence.   Scripture in Romans 11 explained a conceited and egotistical perspective, which resulted in "taking without giving." The character of an engrafted branch illustrated the idea. Paul said, "You do not support the root, but the root supports you." A grafted branch does not support the root, which nourishes its life, but the root supports the engrafted branch. The grafted branch may live, grow, produce foliage and even fruit, but remains an unorthodox part of the larger unit. It often becomes militant and radical and is a liability to the original unit. The graft may also become a hindrance to growth and fruit bearing by sapping strength from the source.

An understanding of the concept of grafting may clarify the problem as it relates to the Christian congregations. One does not have to be a horticulturist to see the disadvantage of foliage without fruit or different kinds of fruit growing on the same tree. Such a fact may be a novelty, but a hybrid has disadvantages. There is something artificial about a hybrid.

A hybrid in plants and animals is the result of the mixing of two different species or varieties. The hybrid may be useful, but it is sterile.   The mule is an animal hybrid produced by interbreeding a donkey and a mare.   It is normally a stubborn animal, which requires a great deal of patience to make useable. When a mixture of culture and faith produces a group, it becomes a kind of hybrid and requires considerable tending to become useful.

When viewed as a whole, Christianity is a mixture of diverse cultures or traditions, and is a hybrid.   The public would consider anything heterogeneous in origin or composition a hybrid organization. It is a composite much as a complicated piece of music of considerable size and complexity.   It takes years of training and practice to translate the music into the harmony intended by the composer. When viewing a Christian congregation, the public cannot see the harmony in the complicated composition.

Perhaps the fig tree has a message. The fig tree was well known and common throughout scripture. They were useful. Adam and Eve wore clothes made of fig leaves. Figs were used as a medicine for Hezekiah. The fruit bearing cycle of the fig tree was common knowledge. The fruit grows on the fig tree before the leaves appear. Consequently, when Jesus was hungry and approached a fig tree in full foliage and found no fruit, He cursed the tree.   Why did Jesus do this?   A tree so full of leaves promised a good harvest of figs.   The application to a Christian congregation is obvious. How do we tolerate a congregation that produces nothing but leaves when the public expects fruit?

When a Christian congregation shows the signs of life and foliage, the public has the expectation that it will produce a harvest of fruit.   When the group sends the wrong message to the public, the consequences will be disastrous. The hybrid organization, which claims deep roots in the Christian Faith, and cannot produce the expected fruit, becomes a stumbling block to the Christian cause.

There will always be differences, but variety does not have to be negative and create disharmony.   A choir is made of different people singing different parts.   This creates harmony.   They are singing the same song in the same key and brought together by the melody. Harmony is a joint exercise.   There is a congruent arrangement of parts, which interweave the different parts into a single whole.   What happened to the common Christian melody that held the early church together?

A musical ensemble is a group constituting an organic whole and together produces a single effect.   There is a careful and balanced integration of the whole performance with no place for a star performance.   The presentation does not permit a single instrument or individual to stand out.   The concept of a choir or an ensemble is the integration of all differences into a single harmony for presentation. The group presents the parts of a musical composition in harmonious agreement.   Unison is the singing of parts in a musical passage at the same pitch and the harmonic combination of two tones an octave apart. This means that a musical scale having eight tones to the octave and using a fixed pattern of intervals can still produce harmony.   With the existing variety in American Christianity, a beautiful melody of spiritual harmony could be projected in unison provided each group could honestly subordinate their religious identity to the common spiritual ground in Christ.

Early Christians had "all things in common."   They were able to gather together in one place in "one mind and one accord" as a family.   The Early Church sang psalms, hymns, and spiritual songs, singing and making melody.

Surely they sang the same songs, in the same key, and made melody in their hearts.   Melody comes from simultaneous musical notes in a chord and produces a pleasing sound. Why then do Christians with only minor differences still produce a mixed message to the general public? Why must we have so many sour notes? Why must the church always use some chromatic half-step scale and make every slight difference stand out as if it were a solo part?

To be viable, the church must make spiritual melody and find true Christian harmony in order to send an appropriate message to the public. Even with many voices there must be one message.   Discord and strife must be overcome. Contention and conflict must cease. The acts and circumstances, which mark the dissension, must be controlled. A lack of harmony and the active quarreling among different groups has become a discordant sound, which strikes the public ear harshly. To make Christianity viable, this must cease.

Christians seem to fight the wrong battles. The conflict over creation and evolution is a good example of a battle lost when the church permitted the deliberation to get to the courts. Evolution was only a theory until a few well-intentioned zealots attempted to force beliefs which some held about scientific creation on the general public.   The consequence of the loss was that public schools across the nation must buy textbooks, which present evolution as fact rather than a theory. California and New York control textbook acceptability. Prior to the legal battle the textbook publishers were careful to present evolution as a theory, not a validated fact. The lesson is clear: the church often fights the wrong battles and in such cases becomes the loser.

The attempt to mandate morality through legislation during the days of prohibition did not work.   Present laws are transparent about misguided efforts. Prostitutes are prosecuted while their clients go free.   Criminal's rights are protected while the victim's rights and privacy suffer. The only hope is for individual Christians to seek common ground and build a bridge to society. Christians must penetrate society and integrate moral and ethical standards to the extent the law permits without compromising principles.

Specific differences should not compromise the areas of general commonalties. Some of the present moral controversy exists over church and state, prayer in the schools, race, abortion, infallibility or inspiration of scripture, as well as the role of public or private education in American life. Morality is not a state prescription or pubic notice by the church. Only individual believers acting in harmony can create a climate conducive to moral and ethical behavior in society.

America has developed an inclination toward separation of God and state through the careless bantering about the separation of church and state. The issue of separation does not mean alienation. The issue has been blamed for a generation of Americans growing up without an adequate moral and ethical standard of behavior. Often problems of teen suicide, pregnancy, drugs, and murder are blamed on the separation issue. This is more likely caused by a separation of God and state, because teen suicides, crime, addiction, and illegitimacy have been a blight on society for years. Some claim these particular teen problems are a result of capitalism rather than secularism. Actually, the church and state split exists superficially as a concept much more than as a functional reality. When the agendas are the same, church and state can work together for the benefit of society. The issue is complicated by the reality that traditional religious liberty and separation of church and state are tied together. The real concern here is religious freedom.

Roger Williams, a Baptist, was the first colonist to advocate separation of church and state, and he was banished from Massachusetts because he preferred democratic government over a theocratic government. He established Providence, RI to foster full religious freedom 140 years before the U.S. Constitution was written. The democratic way of life can be traced back to the Reformation. Today, many have banished the rich heritage of religious freedom. This requires denial of the inspiring history of America's spiritual forefathers who risked their lives and fortunes for religious liberty.

The state was not established to be free from religion; it just cannot take sides in the sectarian controversy which rages over cultural and faith issues. Religious groups which cannot agree among themselves are the best argument for the separation of church and state. Some do not understand that the government staying out of religion is the only security for individual freedom of religion.

In a pluralistic society, the government cannot support a certain religion or endorse a specific denomination or embrace a sectarian doctrine. What is the problem? The problem is simply that Americans want the state to undergird Christianity while the church membership neglects both the church and the state. Some Christians do not vote, or participate in large numbers in volunteer organizations; some do not exhibit high moral character or become spiritual and moral role models. While the church argues about issues of little importance to society, the problems are left to the police, the courts, the foundations, and the Para-church or non-profit groups to deal with the needs of society.

Is the difficulty really prayer in the public schools? Perhaps the question should be about prayer in the home. The Christian conversion experience should have been sufficient to bring spiritual formation into the home. Christian parents should not abandon the teaching of prayer to the state or to individuals from a religion different than their own. The church has not adequately taught parents the responsibility of preparing their children for participation in public school.

During the early years, no one has more influence on children than parents do. The public school teacher should not assume this responsibility. Can the church afford to provide one more excuse for parents to neglect their parental responsibility? A few more excuse feathers could break the back of organized religion and cause it to collapse inward upon the unsuspecting and uncommitted participants.

The issue of race is also dividing local congregations. When good people differ on such crucial social issues, it points out the differences in the Christian community. Jimmy Carter faced such a dilemma in his home church in Plains, Georgia. His difficulty was that politically and personally he could not abide segregation, but he did not wish to quit his lifetime habit of worship with a particular church. In his inaugural address as Governor of Georgia, Jimmy Carter said, "No poor, rural, weak or black person should ever have to bear the additional burden of being deprived of the opportunity of an education, a job, or simple justice." He further declared that the time for racial discrimination was over. This was not true of his local church and it posed a great dilemma for this conscientious Christian. The pastor was dismissed over the issue. A new church was initiated because of the issue. For a time, Jimmy Carter tried to keep his ties with his home church, but after his years in the White House, he began to worship with the other more tolerant congregation.

The racial issue is more about culture than race, more about taught prejudices than honest human differences. Notwithstanding these clear facts, race remains a problem in America and in the churches. The issue still divides some that claim to be Christians. Once divided, the next event is often to be conquered. Does the church have a future in America if it is not inclusive? Did God not make of "one blood, all nations?"

Can there ever be agreement on abortion? Can selfish individuals take a moral position unfamiliar to the rest of their lives? This issue in American life is an example of both the conflict of language and the conflict of an ethical philosophy. Everything that is immoral cannot be outlawed in a civilized society; neither can one accept that everything legal is morally right. Both sides can easily set up a no win, either/or situation for the other side when the language and the culture do not permit such a distinction. The partial birth question has been a no win issue for both sides of the abortion issue. The life or health of the mother, the issue of rape and incest create a middle ground, which blurs the morality of the issue.

The Christian church, by dogma, tradition, sermon, and pontification on the issue, created the no win situation. Reality for most people is clear on some aspects of the issue and blurred on others. Is there a difference in destroying 3,000 fertilized eggs, aborting one twin or 1,3,5,7 or even 8 of octuplets? Most Americans do not choose to make such a decision for another. Some suggest that only the mother could make the choice. Others say the state must control the issue. This is a no win issue in American politics and a controversial issue among Christians. It is an ever-present social issue in each community and in many families. Yet, the decision to let others decide weakens the core of religious beliefs and the moral and ethical standards of society. The same is true of many other issues on which both the church and the state take positions. This is one of the reasons why Christianity does not work well in America.

The battle over the Bible is basically one of an academic argument over a ministry argument. Since the original autographs of the scripture are not available for examination, it is academic to argue for infallibility of the original script. This may be an excellent mental exercise for young academics studying for the ministry, but it has no place in the pulpit. When under-educated ministers or honest laymen attempt to deal with the concept of infallibility of scripture, they are over their heads. Truth cannot be affirmed without facts. Since no data exist, it is really a ministry argument based on the premise that the scripture is inspired and trustworthy for today. It is a matter of faith, not facts. It is the ministry argument that becomes the basis for evangelism and missions.

One does not attempt to explain the academic arguments used to support Christianity in these efforts. The trustworthiness of scripture and the love and concern of a personal God are the issues which count. When the church abandons the ministry argument for an academic one, it is simply preaching to the choir or the deacon bench; the general public is not listening.

Deep in the history of medicine is the concept of bleeding. It was a custom to cut and bleed individuals when they were sick to eliminate the bad blood. The barbershop was an early place for this practice. This is the reason for the red in the old barber pole outside the shop. Even the practice was used on President Lincoln after he was shot in the head. Could medical science have been so ignorant? The Old Testament clearly said, "The life of the flesh is in the blood." It is obvious the medical profession or the public did not understand this adequately.

It took many arguments in the medical community and considerable medical research to establish the true nature of blood as a source of life. Medical procedures championed for years are discontinued when new interventions are available. Can the church afford not to be both practical and innovative in dealing with the basic moral and ethical character of humans and their interaction within society?

There is scriptural precedent for both the academic and the ministry argument. It is found in the two listings of the lineage of Jesus. One lineage traces the ancestry of Jesus back from Mary and another traces the ancestry back from Joseph. One related to the acceptance of Jesus as the Messiah for those who had not yet understood the concept of the Virgin Birth. The other lineage permits the academics to trace back from the mother, which is the basis for the Virgin Birth doctrine. Medical knowledge did not exist at the time to explain that the blood of a fetus comes from the father. Later when it was recognized, the child took the father's family name. Inheritance laws are based on that fact.

With this academic data, one can successfully argue for the Doctrine of the Virgin Birth. Yet, it is an academic argument. That is the argument of St. Matthew, Jesus was King of the Jews; the argument of St. John, Jesus was Divine; yet, St. Luke presents Jesus as a man and St. Mark presents the Savior as a servant. There is room for both the academic and the ministry arguments, but the general public today, just as in the days of Jesus, needs the simple facts of the ministry argument: the written scripture is trustworthy as an inspired oracle of God to present Jesus to the world. Anything else is confusing and counter productive.

Can abandoning the public school or putting Christian kids in church-run elementary and secondary schools without adequate staff or curriculum reform education?

Do congregations have the funds to do this? Is the goal to establish a dual system of education: a secular humanist one operated by the state, and a religious one within the control of the church? If this is the objective, what about taxes, tithes, and tuition? Can the poor afford to pay taxes in support of the public school and tithes in support of the church ministries, then be charged tuition for "saving" their children from the secular humanists? Where does this leave the poor who hear the gospel willingly? Will they be abandoned to a godless system? Where is the battlefront in these matters? Perhaps it is in the home and not in the church. Perhaps in the hearts of honest parents rather than the hands of the preachers or the courts. Perhaps in the concerted effort of concerned individuals rather than the church or state. The answer may be the choice between the lesser of two evils.

An overwhelming number of Americans believe religion is important in their lives. Polls verify that about 90 percent of Americans are religious and have some religious affiliation. Nearly 90 percent believe in a personal God who can answer prayer. Some 84 percent of the polling sample believed that God still performs miracles. Tragically most of those who are religious do not participate in scheduled services presented by organized religious groups. Other research claimed that Americans are less likely to attend church, but they are not turning away from religion.

In one study, 60 percent of the people claimed membership in a local religious institution, but only 42 percent actually attended church. Actually, church membership has declined since 1950. This decline has become a negative participation vote against the status quo, but little has changed. Local churches constantly seek new worshipers with little or no regard for those not present. If notice is taken of the absentee's negative participation it is often rationalized by comment: "they were not of us or they would not have departed..."

Obviously, most Americans prefer to maintain their faith in God, the Bible, prayer and even miracles without regular participation in scheduled services. If the general public has these beliefs, where does that leave the local church? Research data shows no effort in place that has checked the decline. Does this mean that local congregations need to find new and different ways of reaching out to build on the basic religious nature of the people? Should the local church choose not to become relevant to the next generation, there would be little hope for an organized religious influence in America. The ability to influence society would once again fall to the effective witness of individual Christians.

More Catholics than Protestants believe that the human soul goes on to a higher level of existence after death, but nearly one fourth of those who consider themselves non-religious also hold that belief. More Protestants than Catholics presume that God performs miracles today. More Protestants than Catholics affirm faith in a personal God who can answer prayer. Although these findings are consistent with past research, the data does not support any change in religious service participation. At first glance, it appears that the more education one has the less they believe, but that is not the case.

The problem seems to be an academic controversy versus a ministry argument. About 45 percent of individuals with a high school education or less believe the Bible is to be taken literally, word for word, compared to 15 percent of those with a graduate or professional degree. Some 21 percent of individuals with a graduate or professional degree believe the Bible is a book of fables, legends, history and moral precepts recorded by man. Only nine percent with a high school education or less hold this belief. This looks bad for the academic controversy over the literal interpretation of the Bible. Yet some 45 percent of individuals with a high school education consider the Bible to be the inspired word of God, compared with 64 percent of college graduates and 62 percent with a graduate or professional degree accept the ministry argument of inspiration of scripture.

Contrary to popular understanding, the higher one goes in education the more likely they will consider the Holy Scripture used by the church to be inspired. This is an unexpected result from a survey taken by an international secular humanist magazine. Gallup took it because they were suspicious of past research. They used the best scientific polling techniques. The results were surprising.

Does this mean that the higher one goes in education the less one may believe the conservative church position of infallibility of scripture, or the more likely one is to believe in the trustworthiness of scripture as to inspiration? What does all this mean? Does it means that the older, more mature one becomes, the more attuned they are to the nature of the divine; consequently, they need an inspired text in which they can trust?

The church has never taken advantage of this aspect of higher education. Those with professional degrees are often more mature and deal daily with the mixing bowl of life. Could this account for their need to believe in the inspiration of the Bible? The professions are the teachers of the next generation. Public school personnel will spend more time with the young than either parents or preachers. The church should seek to utilize the older and the wiser as a means of reaching the next generation. The church must not abandon higher education to the secular humanist while the church concentrates on the elementary and secondary level as a primary effort to save the next generation.

When more college graduates and individuals with graduate and professional degrees score higher than individuals with a high school education in accepting the Bible as the inspired word of God, one cannot blame the problems in churches on education. It means that higher education has not been the cause of the church losing influence, but one of abandonment of higher education to a minority of secular humanist. Sadly then, education is used as an excuse for some of the problems that confront Christian congregations.

Without a strong academic voice in the classroom of higher education, the church will continue to permit the secularists to influence the teachers of both today and tomorrow. The CHURCHES, the local congregations, and individual Christians must accept responsibility for failure to reach the poor with the gospel and adequately influence higher education in the direction of faith. The basic faith is still there, the church has been unable to take advantage of the opportunity. Too often the church has looked at the negative instead of the positive aspects of higher education. The church should use the ministry argument of inspiration and advance Scripture as a tool to bring morality and ethics back into American society. The spiritual needs of those in higher education must not be abandoned to the secular state. The church has a continuing responsibility to higher education.

While the Bible may be getting some respect in higher education, it is being neglected in the home. Research supports that the Bible has been reduced to an icon and has little practical use in the American home. Not only is the Bible neglected, most Americans lack biblical literacy. Many do not know basic facts from the Bible, which they have heard all their lives. Almost 65 percent of Americans do not know that John 3:16 refers to a passage about believing in Jesus for eternal life. Many confuse old sayings with scripture and are unclear about most of the facts. A few thought the beatitudes were the wives of the disciples and that Joan of Arc was the wife of Noah.

The excuse is a lack of time, difficulty in understanding Scripture, and that it is not relevant to their daily lives. This speaks directly to the lack of relevance for the local church. The truth is that those who attend worship services regularly and listen to preachers almost every week are included among those without biblical literacy. Clyde Reid (1962) said the American pulpit was empty, because no one was listening. No one would have believed the matter could get worse, but it has. Many Christian congregations have lost touch with the people. No one is listening. Even those present find ways to avoid hearing the message.

The world is filled with sounds one never hears because of the limited auditory range of the human ear. Modern man is so assaulted by sound that many and sometimes most sounds are tuned out. Sound is a kind of fourth dimension. All sounds are witnesses of events taking place at the moment. Everything that moves makes a sound. Thus, sound before sight or touch tells one what is going on in ones personal space. Sound reveals complexities that vision alone normally misses. Hearing is an outgrowth of the sense of touch, the most personal of senses. Consequently, hearing is a personalized way of touching at a distance. As such, hearing is the most social of the senses and has particular meaning in the context of collective worship in a gathered church.

Some worshipers, attuned to auditory evaluation, possess the ability to enter a place of worship and through the sounds encountered assess the mood, pace, and direction of the gathered congregation. This is both an asset and a liability to the local church. Provided the worship is sincere and the spiritual leadership honestly communicating from the heart, the visitor and the regular congregants are moved to participate in the process of responding to the spiritual. However, in a congregation filled with strife, confusion, disagreement, a visitor and other participants can soon discern the nature of the gathering and extricate themselves quickly from the association. There is a story of a country preacher seeing a dog in the church isle and asking a deacon to remove the animal. After the sermon, someone told the minister that it was the Seeing Eye dog of a blind visitor. When the preacher apologized, the visitor said, "Oh, that's OK, that sermon wasn't fit for my dog to hear any way!"

Scripture declared that the time would come when men would have ears to hear and hear not. That day has arrived. Even those who attend the worship service do not listen. They invent ways to block out the message, because to truly hear would require action. Three levels of "hearing" have been identified: 1) the level of non-hearing: the sound is heard, but not the words. 2) The level of hearing: the words are subconsciously recorded in the short-term memory, but the meaning and value are not considered. In such cases, the mind, as a tape recorder, may play back the words just as they were received without an awareness of the meaning. 3) The level of listening: the individual receives the words, considers the meaning, and acts on the basis of the meaning to the individual. At the level of listening, one is compelled to respond and therefore act. When worshipers do not listen to the injunctions and challenges from the pulpit, there is little if any Christian action in society.

Politicians and clergy are weak surrogate proclaimers for the morality and ethical stands on social issues. Most Americans put both politicians and clergy at the lowest level of professional credibility. It is people who should be speaking out about the issues that effect their lives and families. Even scripture warned that the "letter of the law kills, but the spirit of the law gives life." Unless America calls a cease-fire on the social and moral issues which plague society, the politicians or the clergy may never put their own houses in order. Without this truce there is little hope of finding workable solutions within a pluralistic society.

The drastic differences in the ethnic and religious background of a pluralistic society hinder the necessary networking of ideas and the webbing of human resources to find acceptable solutions to the sickness which plagues American society. There is hope, but little probability of a cooperative effort in time to save the current situation. The big question is clear: can organized religion be restored to a worthy place in American society? A corollary question begs an answer: can the American government of the people, by the people, and for the people become restored to the point that excesses can be eliminated and the values of government are appreciated? Unless the Christian church reclaims its place of influence on the moral lives of the people, a productive outcome of any action by church or state is doubtful.

The pluralism of American society is secondary at times of national crisis or celebration. Citizens join together during wars and times of crisis to restore peace and tranquility to the country.   After National Elections, for a moment, the political parties lay aside differences and affect a peaceful transfer of power. Individuals rise above petty differences to the commonalties of citizenship. It would assist the cause of Christianity if Christian congregations would present themselves as a community of faith rather than a signpost for name brand religion and frustrate the melting pot process that brings about integration and acceptance of differences for the welfare of the whole.

III. CONGREGATIONS FAIL TO ADVANCE A MELTING POT

Churches produce a stew pot, not a melting pot.

The ethnic and culturally based denominational structure of Protestantism contributes to the American stew pot. Trying to be all things to all men, the church fails to demonstrate the central idea that the good news of the gospel is for everyone. The little kingdoms established to protect a particular cultural expression of religion sends the wrong message to the masses.

A failure to agree on doctrine and polity contributes to the mixed message and suggests exclusivity for most congregations. The unintended message is one of exclusion. The true intent of inclusion is lost in the subliminal message of the architecture, the program, and the general atmosphere of the local congregation.

America was once thought to be the great melting pot of the world where all races, creeds, and cultures could become blended into a pristine commonality. This was called the American dream. One wonders if it were ever a realistic goal.   The difference between a dream and a goal is an agenda. No workable plans existed to produce the melting pot. The Statue of Liberty invited the teaming masses of the world to the shores of America. They came, but they brought their race, creed, culture, and personal dreams. The big dream took a back seat to private aspirations. Everyone was busy building a private fantasy; the corporate dream became a nightmare and a slow and agonizing disillusionment. Private aspirations mostly related to success and providing a better life for the next generation became the common agenda.

Diplomats and politicians spoke of life, liberty, and the pursuit of happiness, but no agenda was provided to bring everyone aboard the American Ark of Liberty. Many were left behind. Some left behind were the guests of Miss Liberty herself: the immigrants. Others were the sick and suffering, homeless and hungry, also the men and women who suffered the wounds of wars were forgotten in the struggle to reach the impossible dream. Those excluded from the marketplace of work or ideas, looked to the church for hope and inclusion.

Could the Christian church become too inclusive? Surely the church would receive everyone in the House of God, but many do not feel welcome. Tragically, in the minds of many, the church gradually became a sanctuary for the charlatan. The House of Prayer became the place to sit and be preached to or preached at, until everyone turned a deaf ear to the message and the messenger. It was as if the people were wandering in a wilderness of mixed messages, false advertising, crooked politicians, broken promises, shattered families, and depleted dreams.

Personal reality has redefined the American dream. America did not become the great melting pot; the United States of America became either a stagnant cesspool or a steaming social stew pot, depending on one's point of view. Some would argue the degradation of the vision needs both the figurativeness of a cesspool and the metaphor of a stew pot adequately to define the current moral and social situation.

A stew pot is a covered pot placed over simmering heat and gradually brought to a low boiling point. Such a stew pot was used by many mothers to prepare nourishing meals for the family, especially during hard times. Despite the stew pot's value in feeding the family, it is the most defining designation for the American Ark of Liberty, because this ark is filled with many distinct kinds of people all mixed and simmering together. Although the people are blended together, there are clusters of identifiable groups and these groups have maintained identify over time. Each item in a stew pot maintains its identity. Potatoes are still potatoes, and so are the carrots, the onions, the celery, and the stew meat itself are all distinguishable. Yet each adds flavor and seasoning to the others. Together they become something more than they were divided.

America is similar in many ways to the stew served on the dinner table. This social stew pot is simmering. The churches of bible days and the churches of history had differences based on cultural and ethnic understandings, but there was sufficient common ground in Christ to bring a sense of fraternity. Each group was permitted to worship God in the framework of their own culture. The church in Jerusalem was different from the church in Antioch. The believers in Corinth were not the same kind of folk as the believers in Ephesus. The countries of Europe managed to maintain a national heritage and these national differences are seen in the churches.

God always reached individuals within the context of personal culture and did not force social change, except in certain aspects of acceptable moral practices. It is clear in scripture that a first-century Gentile did not have to become a Jew to embrace the Christian way. Likewise, a Hebrew did not have to give up the Jewish heritage to accept Jesus as the Messiah. In diversity there is understanding and in commonalties there is strength.

Individuals in a marriage contract remain culturally attached to the family of origin while establishing a new entity and family identity. Likewise, various cultural and ethnic groups within America maintained differences at some levels, but unity at the ultimate measure of devotion to democracy. In many respects, the nation has been more effective in this area than the churches. Why must minor differences in doctrine and polity that are culturally based keep different churches from embracing the common ground in Christianity?   The birth pangs of Protestantism was simply "the just shall live by faith." Why now must the church be divided by different books of discipline and polity? Since there is only one Lord and one Faith, why not a single book of discipline and teaching? Would it be so hard to agree on basic tenants? What about a book of common hymns or a book of common prayers?

President Jimmy Carter had some difficulty with the press and others when he attempted to explain the diversity of the American population. Carter expressed a belief that life was not always fair, and argued for the right of different cultural and racial groups to maintain their ethnicity. Scholars agree with President Carter that the music, art, language, food, clothing, and other aspects of ethnic culture and religious expression are important to each group. Ancestry, history, and social background are all a part of one's heritage. Americans are proud of both their heritage and their differences.   These make the United States of America a strong and viable democracy. Why do religious leaders, who are enjoined to even "love their enemies" and to "pray for those who despitefully use them", not find strength in the common elements of diversity? Why can they not agree to disagree agreeably and move forward with a common message?

Scholars admit the existence of a cultural lag when one part of a population fails to keep pace with the changes in another related aspect, such as the advances in technology and science. Cultural lag and limited education could explain some simmering in the stew pot. Ethnicity and culture are better explanations for the differences in groups than race or religion. Not only do these areas explain some differences within the population of the country, research has confirmed that ethnic, cultural, or national origins are also underpinning elements in denominational differences in America. In reality, the American church has become a product of the pluralistic society.

Just as the foundation stones of democracy and capitalism have been both an asset and a liability to the American dream, the church has been plagued by the diversity that comes from ethnicity or national origin. In a pluralistic society the dichotomy is often the rich and the poor, the employer and the employee, the landlord and the lodger. The dichotomy suggests that America is a house divided, and that is an unstable condition. The church is no less divided: one Lord, one Faith, one Baptism-- but 300 plus CHURCHES. Within these CHURCHES, it has been suggested that more than 21,000 different interpretations of basic Christian doctrine exist. It appears that both America as a Nation and Christianity as a whole, are simmering stew pots. The melting pot theory has not been validated.

Protestant churches emerged in America as a by-product of ethnicity and social pluralism. No acceptable national Christian identity has ever existed; consequently, the Nation was built more by the forces of democracy, capitalism, and global crisis, than upon an underpinning based on the faith of the founding fathers. The Christian trumpet is sounding so many different calls from so many corners that the people do not know where to assemble. Will anyone follow an uncertain trumpet to battle? When the National resolve was limited and the mission was unclear, many refused to follow the Military into Vietnam. The same reaction happened regarding terrorism and Iraq. The same is true for the American church. Even rats desert a sinking ship. Politicians are concerned about popularity and ratings. What is the rating of the church by the general population?

Why has the church been unable to reach successive generations? Perhaps it is because of cognitive dissent among the constituency of Christianity. Many do not believe what their church teaches. Faith inside the church is not much more than a kind of sanctified patriotism to a sectarian denomination. In some areas, basic faith about life and living is higher among those who do not attend church. In fact some clergy, who are required to sign theological statements regularly, do so with mental reservation. Cognitive dissent although passive in nature is militantly aggressive in its effect on the advance of the church.

Management theory presents the dangers of leaders failing fully to agree with corporate or group goals. Even the slightest hint that the leader does not embrace a particular position will be recognized and will have an ill effect. In fact, this kind of dissent is discernible by the senses; it cannot be hidden. Many people have a kind of intuition when a little voice inside speaks up and warns them of inconsistencies in the lives of spiritual leaders. The church itself is a kind of stew pot of beliefs and practices that are not always understood by the public.

There are mixed motives among those who attend church and mixed messages coming from the pulpits. The multiplicity of messages with the miscellaneous meanings has so confused the teachings of the church until accepting the faith of the fathers is difficult for the young. In fact, even the rationale for the word "believe" has changed; instead of expressing faith, at times it expresses doubt or uncertainty. For example, when one is not sure of the weather the uncertain prediction could be "I believe it might rain." When one gives direction, but is doubtful about the details, the explanation could be, "Go three lights, no, I believe it is four. Then turn left for two blocks, no, I believe it is three . . . "Who could follow such direction? This is exactly what the public is hearing from the various churches. "Come here; go there. Go this way; go that way. Do this; do that. Just believe. Give up... turn loose...hold on. Pray and believe. Wait on the Lord. Confess. Be baptized. Join the church. Just believe!" These are unrealistic expectations not related to biblical reality. The early approach to evangelism was based on friendship. Individuals would bring their family and friends to Christ. It is no wonder the scripture explained that one does not come to Christ without the assistance of the Holy Spirit. One would need divine assistance to make any sense out of the mixed message given by Protestant Christianity.

Protestant Christians are caught up in the notion that their denomination has built a better loading ramp for the Old Gospel Ship than anyone else. Consequently, they preach an exclusive message that reaches only a few. It seems that some "believe" their particular plan will work wonders and cause secular society to beat a path to their church door. Others think a specific interpretation of a theological construct is so precise and correct that if it were taught everyone would believe. Some have a kind of theology of coercion that permits almost any effort or procedure to get someone to agree to a specific approach. A recent New England congregation, in their zeal to reach the inner city, was taken to court because a neighborhood claimed, "They were bribing the kids with pizza."

The American family has become a stew pot. Parents are one reason the present generation has turned off the mixed message of the church. The hypocritical lifestyle, the blatant immorality, the obvious unhappiness, all express the failure of the family unit. Since families are the building blocks of the church, the family is a reflection of the church itself. When controversy and friction are present in the home, it complicates the witness of Christianity.

When only one parent is interested in the Christian way of life, children are further confused. Children often think if being a Christian is so great surely dad would be interested. In fact, believers having children by unbelieving spouses have produced a kind of contaminated generation. This infection has grown into a social epidemic of drugs, gangs, and savage violence. The intensity of family dysfunctions has changed both society and the church. The stew pot is simmering.

St. Paul wrote to an immoral church in a depraved society and identified part of the problem. The Corinthian church, the most immoral of the congregations described in the New Testament, was given Paul's personal evaluation about the problem of believers living with unbelievers. It was apparent to Paul that Christian converts must sanctify or "separate" their unbelieving spouse from the immorality of the Corinthian society or their children would be under a serious strain. Paul used the Greek grammatical construction (perfect indicative passive) form for the word "separate." Paul clearly asserted a fact that the action of separation from the immorality of Corinthian society had been a process and was completed; consequently, the next generation would be saints. This was an expression of hope for the future generations.

Paul was predictive of the quality of the children of two parents following the same consecration. His assertion was that they would be blameless and consecrated worthily to be called saints. Even in the midst of an immoral society, Paul believed the next generation could be reached with the gospel. Is this not an indictment against the despair rampant in the church? Since the church has given up on the next generation, where does the church begin to carry out the Great Commission to make disciples?

The implied injunction was that Christians should not be forced to live with unbelievers unless the spouse was willing to separate from the immorality of society. Otherwise, it would bring anxiety and controversy within the home because the unbelieving mate did not share the consecration of the spouse. Without this reformation in the life of the unbelieving spouse, living together as husband and wife would produce children that would be difficult to convert to Christianity. Could this be one explanation for the evils of the present generation and the difficulty the church has of reaching them with the gospel?

Many Christians unintentionally hinder conversion of the next generation by their lifestyle and general attitude about religion and spiritual things. It is the continuing effect of the American stew pot as it boils over into the church. The emphasis on difference is appropriate, but little changes. The church calls for conversion, a total change of mind, heart, and lifestyle, but most things stay the same. There is little difference in the simmering mess in the church and the American stew pot. The church is filled with mixed messages, exploited motives, deceitful manners, manipulated memories, and dysfunctional members. This leads to fraudulent marriages and a restricted ministry of outreach. Morally and ethically the public sees little difference in church members. This lack of significant difference actually hinders the united voice of the Christian church and weakens any effort to reach the younger generation.

The uncertain call of the gospel trumpet does not rally the troops within the church or cause much concern outside the walls. Worship has degenerated to entertainment to attract attendance, but the church cannot compete with television, movies, or the Internet surfers. Christian terminology has not been defined by action. Also, the social stew pot has allowed cultural interpretations to divide the various groups of Christians based on the cultural interpretations of church teachings. Another factor is that the theological constructs of the church have been placed in the ambiguity of the English language that has an either/or complex and leaves little room for middle ground in matters of faith and practice. This leads to a lack of inclusiveness; in fact, it bred exclusivity and eliminated many from the influence of the Christian lifestyle.

Just as the biblical Israelites, the American church has become sidetracked in the pluralistic wilderness on the way to the American dream. The Israelites wandered for forty years until all of the disobedient generation died, and then the next generation was permitted to cross into the Promised Land. Journeying out of Egypt the Israelites witnessed the miracles of God. Based on the promises of God regarding deliverance, the bones of Joseph were taken from Egypt to the family burial site across the Jordan, but the people were denied entrance to the land that flowed with milk and honey. This denial came because of fear and timidity: fear of the walled cities and the giants in the land and timid in claiming the promises of God to give them the land.

Twelve spies were sent to evaluate the possibilities. Ten came back with a report of gloom and despair. Two claimed that Israel and the God of Israel were well able to possess the land. The majority refused to take the enabling step of faith and behave, as the Children of God should act: take the first step by faith in the direction of the promise and claim victory. Joseph had done just that many years before. At his death Joseph reminded the Israelites that God would visit them and deliver them safely to the Promised Land. Joseph made it. Joshua and Caleb, the two spies with the minority report, made it. Those who would not act wandered as the People of God, but perished in the wilderness without claiming their promised possession. This sounds a little like the American church.

Many Protestant churches are marked by frustration, mediocrity, failure, and wandering in the wilderness of a secular society. Public sins, private defeat, abject loneliness, broken relationships and paralyzing depression characterize the church membership. Yet, there are a few such as Joshua and Caleb who give the minority reports. We are well able to take the land. God uses the weak. God uses the child. God uses the small and insignificant things to effect His purpose provided those God chooses to use are willing to take the risk and make the steps of faith.

The social stew pot of America has pushed the equality of individuals.   Minorities and women have been given certain advantages in an effort to overcome generations of white male domination. Just a few years back it could be said, "It is a man's world".   Although Christianity liberated women and made a claim that "In Christ there was neither male nor female, bond or free", the New Testament era was one of slavery and male dominance. In fact, the church took the cue from the society of the day and created a male leadership. Only a few women were able in the early days to secure opportunities for ministry and leadership within the church. However, as society began to push the equality button, the church jumped on the bandwagon.

The willingness of the church to accept more female leadership grew more out of a lack of men than an effort to advance women. Notwithstanding the actual reasons for opening the door to women, there has developed a kind of feminization of the church. This sends the wrong signal to men, who are already in short supply. The message, although unintentional, communicates that the church can get along without men. This is no more the case than it is in the family.

Some families survive without a father, but the message to the children is confused as to the role of a father. This complicates ones view of God the Father. Research demonstrated that one normally attributes the same qualities to God the Father as are attributed to ones biological father.   Growing up without a father has complicated evangelism in the inner city. On one effort, the literature had to be changed to place an emphasis on Jesus as the Big Brother rather than God as Father. The church must be careful in the effort to give women a rightful role in advancing the church; care must be taken to send the right message to men.

Failure of the church to take some of the responsibility for the failure in families also complicates the problem. The bitterness and alienation within the dysfunctional family is normally transferred to the church. Often people in the church take sides when a marriage is dissolved. This multiplies the problems of the two families already caught in the confusion of broken contracts, failed relationships, wounded children, and divided observers who watch, take sides, and shout advice as if they were at some sporting event. This creates wounded and scarred individuals who do not feel they can turn to the church for comfort or sanctuary. The church purports to be a place filled with mercy and understanding, but the steaming stew pot clouds the manifestation of these virtues; consequently, the image of the House of God is tarnished. Often the most grievous wounds are received in the house of friends. It has been said that the church is the only army that shoots its wounded. Certainly the action of many creates a pessimistic atmosphere in which forgiveness is difficult.

This lack of forgiveness contaminates the soul of the congregation. Many wounds received in relationship battles leave psychological scars that affect the self-concept of the wounded. This often causes both individuals and groups affected by the war of words to hold animosity and bitterness for years. When this occurs, everyone, including the ministry of the church, endures great affliction. It becomes clear that the family, the community, and the church are interrelated, and what happens in one impacts the others. Each individual is affected by the larger society and by each other. As the family goes, so goes the church. When the community deteriorates, the church usually follows. When families are strong, the church is strengthened, and communities become better places in which to live and bring up children.

The whole issue of brand names for churches is confusing. So many different Baptist churches: American, Southern, Independent, Free Will, Conservative, Primitive, Missionary, Regular, General Baptists and the names go on and on. Other Protestant CHURCHES have various qualifying names as well. There is the Presbyterian Church (USA), Presbyterian Church of America, Cumberland Presbyterian, etc. Then there are United Methodists, Wesleyan Methodists, Evangelical Methodists, and Free Methodists. The Restoration Movement did not intend to start a denomination but ended up with the Christian Church, Church of Christ, Disciples of Christ, plus independent Christian churches. Some denominational identities have as many as twenty different qualifying factions. How can the general public make any sense of this diversity?

There are sound reasons for the names given to churches, but many add to the bewilderment. The confusing names add more heat to the simmering stew pot. One sign said Temple Chapel Church; another Protestant congregation in a Jewish area called itself Bethesda Temple. Other use such names as Full Gospel, Free Will, Evangelical, Evangelistic, House of Prayer, Temple, Tabernacle, Cathedral, Chapel, Mission, Meeting House, and then there are such specialized names as the Greater Baptist

Sanctified Holy Church of the First Born Missionary Tabernacle, Incorporated. There seems to be no limits to the length some will go to create an uncommon identity. Then there are churches that have the same name, but have different doctrine. Although there are honest reasons behind the choice of names, the lack of commonality baffles the general public. Just how does this fit into the concept of one Lord, one Faith, and one Baptism?

Yet, in the midst of the confusion there are a few individual churches that have prevailed. They are growing, reaching out, sending missionaries, and growing a new generation of Christians. These few churches seem to have the old American "can do" attitude, the vast opportunities are seen and the courage and faith to work together in the Name of Christ is working. Just how many and how long this will work cannot be predicted, but these have crossed the social Jordan of despair, breached the immoral walls of the secular cities, and embraced the inhabitants as redeemed friends. These few have claimed their community as their parish and are ministering grace to all who will receive. The organized church has problems as a whole, but individually there is hope!

There are both social and political aspects to forms of religious ceremony and etiquette observed in the community. Participants from a civil perspective may see a particular religious ceremony as a secular event. Notwithstanding the failure to see the true religious nature of certain social events, individuals, families, and society as a whole benefit from the stabilizing forces on society. The event may actually perform a social role and be a stabilizing force in society without the individuals seeing the religious significance of the process. Some do not see religion as a part of their personal life, but they see religion playing a social role, dignifying and making an event acceptable or traditional.

 Those who see or use the church in this manner do not feel a need personally to belong or participate in the regularly scheduled religious activities of a local congregation. Somehow the church must go beyond contributing to the civil culture of the community and develop a Christian culture that can influence the personal behavior of the community.

IV. CONGREGATIONS FAIL TO ATTEST PERSONAL BEHAVIOR

Churches promote activities rather than behavior.

The church fails to bear witness to the Christian behavior appropriate for those who claim membership. There is no effort to certify moral and ethical behavior as a model; in fact, the behavior of many church related folk suggest that the opposite is acceptable. Positive role models are absent, and little effort is made to support those who rise above the standards of society. The public receives more information on "heroes" and "champions" from the sports arena and the secular press than from the church.

An agenda of scheduled group activity pervades the American church. This negates the power of personal behavior so essential to advancing the Christian cause in any culture. The true means of advancing Christianity is not rooted in institutional activity regardless of how well they are planned and executed. The practical theology expressed in organizational activity may be an important aspect of congregational life, but it is not the most effective means of advancing the Christian faith. The practice of formal public worship, program administration, preaching, and pastoral care may be essential to the operation of the local church, but these activities are not the substance of the Christian faith. Scheduled activities may demonstrate the ability of leadership to organize, but do not point to the strength of the individual. In fact, most of the activity exists because of failure at the individual level. When only paid staff and surrogate witnesses are heard by the public, the essence of Christianity is lost. If no individual sensitivity for the personal witness exists in the community, then the church has failed to prepare the people for a proper life style.

The gathering together of individuals in public worship for encouragement and education is an important aspect of the corporate life of the Christian family; however, this gathering must never be considered a substitute for the personal action and involvement incumbent on each believer. Many of the ills of the human family could be traced to a lack of activity and time spent in the sitting position. Man was structured to stand up, walk and work until he was tired and then to lie down and rest until he was able to work again.   Why then is man physiologically permitted to sit down? Research suggested the mobility was for versatility so man could walk and work. This physiological versatility has been misused to sit down; spectators in the seated position with little or no meaningful activity. Could this be part of the problem at church?

There is something about the sitting position which alters the pressure on vital organs and causes physical problems. Certainly the work habits of modern man differ from those of primitive ancestors. It is also true that the nature of the church in the modern world is different than the operation of early Christianity in a more primitive and less complex society. Certainly things are much more complicated in modern society.

Notwithstanding the obvious, could the lack of personal activity, combined with organized group activities which require a passive sitting position in church, be the source of some of the spiritual problems in the Christian community? Many who have endured the length of a religious service somehow feel they have done their "service" to God and man and that nothing else is required. There is a story about a preacher who preached too long, but during the sermon he explained the bandage on his chin. "While shaving this morning, I was thinking about my sermon and cut my chin." Afterwards, a woman suggested that the next time he should think about his chin and cut his sermon. A story out of old England speaks to this issue. It seems the church was honoring the fallen soldiers who died in wartime service. Not fully understanding the ceremony, a small boy asked his mother if the soldiers died in the morning or evening service.

Christianity has become church-*ianity* and developed an excessive sectarian attachment to the practices of a particular cultural view of the church. The form of government has become more important than the effective operation of the church. The function of the congregation may change according to the government, but the purpose of a Christian congregation would be the same regardless of church polity. Does it really matter if a church has elders, deacons or stewards? Does the effective witness of a local church differ if it has a congregational government or is part of a connectional denomination? It is doubtful that the form of government will change the population of Heaven.

The Christian sacrament of baptism is marked by confusion. Within the Christian community the observance of baptism is used for different reasons and performed by different methods. For some it is an act of purification, for others one of separation, still others see water baptism as an act of initiation or identification. Notwithstanding the purpose of baptism, the mode is of more concern to some than the actual purpose of baptism or the obedience to Christ's command. Controversy actually exists over whether the baptismal water may be still or must be running. Will the population of Heaven be changed by the mode of baptism? Are these differences sufficient cause to divide the body of Christ? Is the mode or the act of obedience on the part of individuals the essential matter? Are these differences and divisions worth the muddled message they send to the public? Can the Christian message be viable when such variation in basic understanding exists among the faithful practitioners? From the viewpoint of eternity, does the method of immersion versus sprinkling make a significant difference?

There is an old story of a Baptist arguing with a Methodist over the mode of baptism: it seems the Baptist insisted on total immersion and the Methodist thought the act of sprinkling as a personal preference was sufficient. They agreed it was not the amount of water, but what the water covered. Water up to the knees, waist, or even to the neck was not sufficient for the Baptist, if the water did not cover the forehead or top of the head it was not a valid baptism. The argument was simple: the water must cover the head.

The Methodist countered, "You mean if the water covers everything on a person but the forehead it is not a sufficient baptism?" The Baptist agreed that unless the forehead was covered it was not a valid baptism. The Methodist contended since covering the forehead was what ultimately counted, the method of sprinkling could be used to be absolutely sure to get the forehead wet. This is a ridiculous story and has little to do with the true value of baptism, but it points out the nature of the difficulty.

The problem is culture, heritage, polity, and practice. Differences exist. They are inevitable, but do not have to divide or weaken the Christian message. Differences of a minor nature could be presented within the local congregation to maintain harmony and unity of a particular local church. Why must dissimilarity be institutionalized and practiced without regard to the distortion it brings to the total Christian message?

The method of organizing and operating church visitation has become more important in some congregations than sharing the gospel with one's neighbor. Driving across town to receive a visitation assignment and then driving back across the city to visit someone else's neighbor is ridiculous. Is this not manipulation: getting someone to do what others want done. It has little to do with the Christian witness and more to do with church programming and attendance building.

The artificial manipulation of personal activity in an attempt to accomplish a spiritual work can never maintain the witness of a Christian congregation. Are there no Christian incentives for involvement? Does no personal motivation or impulse to Christian activity exist in the church? Must the church arrange all religious activity? Does the internal change which comes with Christian conversion not require the individual to be personally involved in sharing the faith with family, friends, and neighbors, -- even enemies? Individual Christians must become involved in the daily sharing of a common faith.

The Christian community suffers when too few attempt to do too much. Advancement of the Christian cause is not the sacred task of a select few. There must be person-to-person involvement. Scripture furnishes ample precedent for a personalized persistent involvement in the market place rather than an occasional activity in the stained glass ghetto of the church. The true nature of New Testament Christianity was determined by a simple pattern. No one waited until Sunday or invited a friend to church to hear a sermon to become a Christian. Every believer felt a part of the priesthood and constantly presented the claims of the gospel to anyone who would listen.

The American church has lost a central idea of Lifestyle Christianity: everyone going everywhere and sharing the gospel with assurance that God would confirm their testimony with spiritual results. This central idea is still valid. Members of Christian congregations can never be mobilized to advance the cause when their only religious activity is attending meetings scheduled by an institution.

Since Christianity is every believer's business every day, to delay personal involvement until some scheduled institutional activity is to forfeit an opportunity to make a difference in society. This act of delay causes Christianity to suffer from the problem of upward delegation.   This is a neglect of individual and personal responsibility for sharing faith on a daily basis.   The upward delegation to professional and paid staff of the church greatly handicaps the mobilization of Christianity and the propagation of a common faith to society.

Industry solved the problem of upward delegation through the technique of a finished task. The simple solution was for each person to complete work without passing the unfinished task upwardly.   The person nearest to the problem would use common knowledge to intervene. It was "Handle it while you have your hands on it." Usually the individual at the point of difficulty was more knowledgeable about the problem than anyone available. Yet, not wanting to assume responsibility for personal action, workers constantly sought the advice and assistance of others concerning minor difficulties.   This upward delegation has occupied institutions with many unnecessary decisions that could be better made at the individual level.

Individuals who have accepted the Christian faith as a way of life must assume responsibility for personal opportunities before the problem of upward delegation can be solved.   This has great significance for the present difficulty in American Christianity. The program to advance Christianity cannot be sent down from the top or brought in from the outside. Each aspect of the program must be adapted and tailored to the culture of the people. This means the program is people responsive; consequently, institutional leaders are unable to structure such programming.   The program should come up from the people to be effective.   It must be in the hands of individual believers and the result of life style choices. The problem seems to be one of too many chiefs and not enough Indians.

Young David in scripture used a sling and five smooth stones to defeat the enemy of Israel.   The shepherd lad could not fight the giant in the armor of King Saul.   The tool must fit the hand of the worker. The worker must be a willing participant in the process.   This can never happen when the institution plans and schedules all the religious endeavors.   Under such circumstances, those attending religious functions feel they have performed some "Christian service", when in reality they have been only an unwilling participant in a scheduled activity.

There is a story of two farmers in competition for the apple market.   One always seemed to get to market first with the most.   The other farmer hired a consultant who discovered the losing farmer had six in the management area and only one apple picker while the winner had only one in management and six apple pickers. So the losing farmer restructured but lost again because he had one general manager, and five section leaders, but only one apple picker. The story concluded with the losing farmer firing the one apple picker and scheduling a meeting of the remaining employees to discuss the problem.   Does this anecdote speak to the institutional infrastructure filled with councils, committees, task forces, and staff with almost no one doing the true work of the church?

Entrenched leaders, regardless of how or why they arrived at their position of authority, often develop into personal stakeholders and make personal adjustments to activities which further complicate the involvement of others. They become comfortable in the way things are handled because the program has been structured to their limitations or convenience. This vested interest becomes a major obstacle to the advancement of Christianity.

Such leaders appear to be walking a treadmill. They are caught in a prison of previous pattern; consequently, there is a great deal of motion without progress. The church staff is hyperactive, but the congregation sleeps like a giant. The church has developed an active shepherd--passive sheep structure with little hope of significant change. Most Christian congregations have adjusted to a mediocrity and have settled for something less than basic Christianity. A Christian congregation is not supposed to be a hospital for saints or a social club for sinners; in reality, the church is to be a ministry of prayer and support for the community of faith. When it fails to be this, it fails.

Pastoral care is the major occupation of the professional staff of a Christian congregation. Time is spent visiting uncle John's-aunt's-brother's-nephew's-cousin, with little results. Yet, the staff persists in the process with the tenacity of the US Mail or a Hollywood Star on stage: "The mail must go through...the show must go on!" Constantly, a dependent congregation "calls" for a visit and expects prompt service from the highest available staff. When they call for the doctor, they do not want to see the nurse. In some cases, pastoral care is called "counseling," but in reality it is not the long-term therapy required to be classified as counseling.   It is normally short term, crisis intervention and requires nothing more than a ministry of presence together with spiritual concern and mentoring. However, an abnormal amount of time and energy are spent that could be used in more productive ways.

Decades ago Clyde Reid (1967) in his work on preaching as communication declared the American pulpit to be empty: The pulpit today is empty in the sense that there is often no message heard, no results seen, and no power felt. The emptiness of which I speak is an absence of meaning, a lack of relevance, and a failure in communication. To be sure, this is a relative emptiness, not absolute. However, it is emptiness, nevertheless.

The empty pulpit has become a half-filled church with half-hearted commitment to the basic tenets of the Christian faith. Any defense of the viability of American Christianity is to say that the structures of the past are good enough for today and the future. This is certainly not true in any other aspect of life or history. A local church is made up of people and people change. Churches exist in a society, and societies change. Change is the one constant factor of modern life. The Christian congregation must become more people responsive. The structure, message and communication of American Christianity must change to maintain any semblance of viability for the future. The quality of individual Christianity must be restored.   Each believer must practice a lifestyle that is a witness to personal faith.

Could a coffee-house ministry in the inner city do a better job of reaching the present generation? What about other alternatives? Could the living room or den of individual Christian homes better serve as a place of worship than the stylized denominational promotion centers called a local church? Churches of the New Testament met in individual member's homes. Some growing congregations have revived this approach to extending the church.   It certainly places the responsibility on individuals and families to bring their behavior into conformity to the Christian faith.

How does the church provide wholesome activities for other days of the week? What about the membership, which never shows up at the scheduled services because of work, sickness, or discouragement? Would the church staff be better off meeting the needs of the absentees than the effort used to satisfy the few attending the public service?

It is the dependency on organized activities rather than personal witnessing that has caused the decline in evangelism.   Many faithful Christians are active witnesses through a lifestyle that puts them in touch with the world. It is the organized church that has failed not individual believers. Members must no longer depend on the scheduled activities of the church to advance the gospel; there must be personal acceptance of individual responsibility for sharing the good news. It will not come from the pulpit sermons, because many that need to hear are not present and those present are not listening. It will not come from the paid staff of churches, because they are so encumbered with organized activities there is no time left for an active witness. Regretfully, even the passive witness of most is tarnished by the paraphernalia of position and the burden of ecclesiastical regulation. The only hope is the personal work of a spiritual laity. An adequate record of the lifestyle evangelism would read similar to the Book of Acts. Such a record would show the effective human participation in the work of God. At the individual level, Christianity is alive. God is no less at work in the world today. Tragically, there are few records of the unnamed saints of the Christian faith who actively share their faith in the marketplace. The only facts known to me are of a personal nature, but they must be shared as an illustration of what has been and what is being done across America to advance the cause of Christ.

The people who need the gospel do not attend the churches. Since this is the case, how then will individuals be brought face to face with the opportunity of saving grace? The only answer is the personal witness of individual Christians who share their faith through a lifestyle witness every day. Such an event took place in my life one January. Each year near my birthday, a personal effort is made to pray, plan, and think about the coming year. What can be done differently? What can be done better? What can be done new that would advance the gospel? During this time of meditation, my impression was to travel to New York City.

Using a credit card to purchase a ticket, a flight was boarded which ended at LaGuardia. A limousine to the hotel and a good nights sleep and then perhaps understanding would come as to why God impressed me to travel to New York. In the bed, almost asleep, the telephone rang. The front desk clerk spoke clearly, Dr. Green come to the lobby, PLEASE." Past ministry had put me in seventeen different churches in the city, but no one knew my plans to be in New York. Quickly, putting by pants over my PJ's, the only thought was to follow directions to the lobby. As the elevator door opened, a man dressed only in pants, no shirt, no shoes, holding a wrecking bar in one hand and a pair of scissors in the other, turned and saw me. "I don't want to be saved," he screamed. At that moment, my mission was clear.

Walking up to the man with an outstretched hand, he gave me his weapons and answered the question about his room number, 506. About this time, the New York police came to make an arrest, but the explanation that the hotel had asked me to handle the situation caused the officer to wait. Agreeing that it was bad whiskey and admitting that a good night's sleep could change things for him, the police agreed to put a guard outside his door. He went to sleep.

Returning to my room on the ninth floor, my heart was pounding. What was God doing? Were there no Christians in New York City willing to reach out to such a person? Must God bring someone all the way from Atlanta to do the work of personal witnessing? My telephone rang again; it was the man. "Are you the gentlemen who helped me downstairs?" With an affirmative answer, he asked for my prayers. Following a brief prayer over the telephone, a wake-up call was scheduled for 6:30 AM, and a planned meeting in the coffee shop at 7:15 AM. Sleep finally came.

The next morning in the coffee shop, the man was asked a simple question about the Bible. "Do you believe this book is the Word of God?" He was unsure, and on follow-up, said he did not know anyone who believed the Bible. Then, as if out of the clear blue, he said, "An old man in Boston a few weeks ago, talked with me about being born again. He believed the Bible! Do you think that born again business would help me?" The door was open; God was working. A simple explanation about believing with the heart and confessing with the mouth was sufficient. It was not a scheduled church activity; it was a personal witness in the marketplace that God used to change this life. A letter confirming that change came in a few days on a Washington, DC Chamber of Commerce letterhead. God does work in mysterious ways to perform His work in the world.

My paternal grandfather was a faithful Methodist who believed and trusted in God. He was a farmer and one year he had a distinguished crop of corn. This story is a practical point about human involvement in the divine plan. It seems that grandfather took a city slicker to see the cornfield and remarked about how proud he was of the crop. The city fellow told grandfather to be grateful to God for providing the land, the sunshine, the rain and that in reality it was God who made the corn grow. After listening to the lengthy exhortation, grandfather retaliated: "I know God is working, but you should have seen that field when God had it by Himself! He sure left a lot of work for me to do."

As a farmer, grandfather had learned from experience what most Christians never learn: God is working, but human beings must also work to harvest a spiritual crop and attain spiritual accomplishments. It is clear;God uses individuals to advance the gospel message; God does not do for human beings those things that they can do for themselves. This speaks to human involvement in God's work in the world. Perhaps the current problems in the American church can be traced to leaving too much for God to do and not accepting responsibility for sharing the gospel with others when God opens the door. When individuals depend too heavily on scheduled church activities, the power of the individual witness is limited.

Traveling alone down Interstate 75 south of Atlanta, the long journey ahead suggested a hitchhiker might be good company. As the young man entered the car he heard, "Good morning, my name is Hollis Green, I am a Christian." The response was, "Carl Krudoff, I am a philosopher." The young philosopher was baited, "Do you write your philosophy down, or do you just talk? He claimed to write important thoughts down. This interested me, so he was asked about his most recent writings. Carl said, "I have just written a definition of God, but I don't believe there is one."

A definition of God by a philosopher who doesn't believe in God; this was going to be interesting. Reaching into the back seat to retrieve a small-unzipped notebook, Carl began to read: *"God is the singular, possessive, abstraction of the adverb."* He was a philosopher; my teachers talked that way. Carl was asked to run the statement by me again. He repeated, **"God is the singular, possessive, abstraction of the adverb."** My unspoken question was, "What is an adverb?" I had been out of school too long. Carl continued, *"An adverb is the linguistic manifestation of a life process."*

It is my firm conviction that God provides both the situation and the supply to share with others the good news. The discussion centered on Carl's definition of God. On close examination, it was good theology. This fact was discussed at length. Carl's use of the present tense initiated dialogue. The singularity of one God was considered. The possessive or jealous nature of God expressed with Israel in the Old Testament was discussed. The fact that God's ways were past finding out centered on Carl's observation about God being the "abstraction of an adverb." It was clear that Carl could not understand the spiritual construct of God and needed to take one step at a time.

Carl was a young intellectual, and somewhere in his comprehension of the use and function of the adverb was the key to an adequate perception of God. Carl's personal definition would be the key; *"An adverb is the linguistic manifestation of a life process."* The God whom Carl defined was not viable to him because there was no systematic order relating the signs and symbols about a Divine Person to a personal reality. In English, an adverb is used to modify a verb, adjective, or another adverb by expressing time, place, manner, degree, or cause. Also, an adverb is used to express action, existence or occurrence; an adjective expresses a quality and defines or describes a noun.

God, in this case, was the big Verb and the big Noun, and Carl had never witnessed the action of God in real time. He needed someone who had personally experienced the power and action of God to adjust the semantics and syntax of the experience to a language he could accept. Carl needed the same touch of experiential reality of the

Crucifixion and the Resurrection that Thomas of scripture desired. Jesus gave Thomas that opportunity. Carl simply needed a touch of first hand experiential reality: a manifestation of the resurrected life of Jesus Christ. At last, the course of action was clear. Carl needed to see one of God's adverbs.

With this awareness, the original introduction was altered and repeated, **"Good morning, my name is Hollis Green, I am one of God's adverbs."** A spark of cognitive ignition occurred, Carl's mind was open, the heart was ready, and the Holy Spirit had done His work. A simple walk down the Roman Road of scripture brought Carl face to face with the reality of the man Christ Jesus. He accepted not only the present tense existence of the Creator God, but a personal relationship with Jesus, the Son. Carl was greeted as a brother, a fellow adverb to go forth and point to the real time action of God.

God works in mysterious ways to perform His work of redemption using human instruments and circumstances. Traveling to Washington, DC during the Vietnam War to intercede for a young soldier man who had been mistreated because of his Christian faith, God opened a door for witness. Just before catching the plane, my schedule took me to a publisher to review the galley proof of a book. While there, an old newspaper was noticed on the floor. Since neatness is a virtue, my decision was to pick up the paper from the floor. I discovered it had been used to cover an ink spill and was stuck to the floor. In the process, a small piece tore off in my hand. It was a picture of a skunk and a story about a farmer.

A Pennsylvania farmer had observed an old skunk for several days. One day the skunk abandoned his old home and dug a new nesting hole. The farmer was intrigued, so he watched. The skunk, with great care, gathered grass and leaves and lined the inside of the excavation. The skunk looked around for what was to be his last glance at the world and then entered the hole. The behavior fascinated the farmer, so he waited. When the skunk failed to come out of the hole, the farmer was curious.

Taking a stick, the farmer punched into the hole. Nothing happened. Finally, he knelt down and raked back the leaves so the skunk could be seen. The skunk did not move; it was dead. The farmer observed that the skunk was old, with broken teeth, and concluded the skunk could no longer hunt for food and had prepared to die. Reading this story seemed foolish at the time, but God had a reason.

Seated about half way back in the coach section of the plane, a young soldier chose the empty seat next to me. As the plane took off, the soldier turned and said, "I probably won't be alive a year from now, I'm on my way to Vietnam." This matter of fact statement jolted my memory of the skunk story. As the story was shared with the young soldier, his face became thoughtful. The time had come for me to present the claims of Christ. If an old skunk had enough sense to prepare to die, surely it would be wise for a soldier going to battle to make preparation to die. His answer, "Sir, I would if I knew how." The door was wide open. The ABC's of the gospel (all have sinned, believe on the Lord Jesus Christ, and confess with your mouth and you will be saved) were presented. The young soldier prayed to receive Christ and went to war prepared to die. God uses spilled ink, old newspaper stories, a plane ride, and a troubled but searching heart to do the work of redemption.

The problem is not that scheduled activities can do no good; it is that the people who really need them are not present. The challenge for the Christian church is in the marketplace, out where the people are on a daily basis. Traveling opens many doors for the gospel. At the airport waiting in line for a delayed night flight, two gentlemen were talking around me in line. When they would not break line, their conversation was forced on me. Understanding their frustration, my Delta Flying Colonel card was used to take them to a more private place to wait.

The Crown Room was almost deserted. Soft drinks were in the refrigerator and little fish crackers on the counter, so the munching started. After a while, one asked, "Do you work for the airline?" A negative answer was not sufficient; the follow up question dealt with my occupation. They were told about my travels, writing and speaking. One asked, "What do you write?" Sharing with them about discipleship, evangelism and dying churches in America, one said, "My church is dead, and I am too!" With this, the other one decided to leave.

Alone, God worked the mysterious process of renewal and commitment. A note on Delta stationary from the Crown Room arrived in the mail. It listed "Seven things God did for me today." Religion is not dead, the cause of Christ is alive and well; it is just functioning better on an individual basis that it is at the organized level. Local congregations must seek to enhance the quality of daily involvement by individual Christians rather than the quantity of attendance on Sunday. The way forward and the effort most likely to succeed is the strengthening of the family. Not just efforts to support family values but a clear action that demonstrates the value of families.

V. CONGREGATIONS FAIL TO AUGMENT THE VALUE OF FAMILIES

Churches embrace family values rather than value families.

The church has failed to adequately influence American families. Church and family life have become part of the American stew pot. Parents are one reason the present generation has turned off the mixed message of the church. The hypocritical lifestyles, the blatant immorality, the obvious unhappiness, all express the failure of the family unit. Since families are the building blocks of the church, the family is a reflection of the church itself. When controversy and friction are present in the home, it complicates the witness of Christianity.

The dysfunctional nature of families within the church is about the same as those in the general public. Although this may speak to the deterioration of society, the church must accept some responsibility for the failure of the family. Does the church not have an obligation to influence families in the direction they ought to go? Is this not the essence of Christianity? The church has been aggressively hypocritical in insisting on family values but not modeling or teaching the value of families. A lack of role models and accountability for failure clearly exists.

American Christians have failed to transmit adequate experiential knowledge of the Christian life to succeeding generations to make genuine converts. This, coupled with the mobility of a pluralistic society, has produced complex and confusing relationships within congregations. Consequently, preachers and parents unintentionally hinder the conversion of the next generation to the Christian faith.   To make local churches viable in the Twenty-first Century, there must be an internal redirection of the protestant spirit that clearly testifies for the faith that is truly believed.   This must be done with less emphasis on sectarianism and parochial adherence to particular CHURCHES, and more emphasis on personal faith and the value of the family unit.

A cultural framework for doctrine created a brand name concept for many Christians in America. This development was based on the writings of past theologians and produced a freeze frame theology not relevant to the present generation.   In some cases, the next generation has a denominational or sectarian orientation rather than exposure to a basic Christian perspective. This together with other compounding factors has complicated the growth and viability of Christianity.

Most congregations are more interested in doctrine and polity than connecting with the local community.   One response to a strong sermon was, "It may be Bible, but it is not Baptist." This kind of narrow-minded adherence to a sectarian position has closed the mind of many to the relevance of the Christian message for the present generation.   There seems to be little "first generation" excitement and acceptance of the message. When the church and community do not join forces to meet the needs of the people, religion has no viability. When the people of a particular community are not open to the basic teaching of scripture, the seeds of failure for the church sprout and grow.

A tragic flaw dividing Christianity is dissimilarity and it presents a misleading message.   When common ground is not accentuated both the church and the community suffers.   This failure heightens the negative effect of the differences rather than the positive results of commonalties. Sadly, this is done as if the process of stating distinctive differences were an asset. In reality it is a drawback to the public understanding of the Christian Faith and a liability to individual and institutional cooperation in areas where there should be a common agenda. Disunity leads to a dysfunctional system.

The church has not become a family advocate. Family values are high on the list of priorities, but little real action is taken. No one will admit they are against family values, because most Americans are concerned about the pressures in society that are undermining many families. Roughly fifty percent of all marriages in American are dissolved, but many more are dysfunctional. It is estimated that the United States may have the highest divorce rate in the world. Some marriages do more harm to the parties, including the children, than a divorce, but the church does little to assist with this difficulty. The church does not adequately advance qualities that make strong family units. This neglect has caused many children to become pawns of the court system.

God produces children into the world through families. Parents, siblings, and extended family members have great impact on the child. Parents who turnover the rearing children to the state or the church abdicate the basic requirements of parenthood. Church and state have a place in the protection of children, but primary care must come from parents and members of the extended family.

The church must reevaluate the role of the family both in the religious education of children and in the spiritual experience of a lifestyle conducive to basic spiritual development. Families have an impact on the total development of children that far exceeds what could be expected given the size and fragile family organization.

The church has neglected family life education. In most cases, the needs of the family do not have a prominent aspect in the program for parents or the children. There is overwhelming evidence that what happens within the family impacts not only the human development of the persons involved but affects the church as well. Children and parents have no organized voice to speak about their specific needs. The church could and should become that voice.

The impact of families on individuals, the church and community, and ultimately the nation has been ignored. Just as the educational system has been preoccupied with curriculum and the teachers union, the church has concentrated on the doctrine and polity of the past without a realistic concern for the present needs of the children and their parents.

A strong consensus has emerged in recent years about the specifics and characteristics of those families who build and assist human and spiritual development versus those different characteristics of families who undermine and destroy the competence and potential of the children. Family life education advanced both by the public education and the church must concentrate on the style of education that meets the needs of the children, and the contexts in which this education can best be done. The church is particularly equipped to assist in this process, but the religious community continues to concentrate on other things.

Families are the smallest and most fragile social group and are often overlooked or taken for granted by the church in an effort to build the institution. Research strongly suggests that the impact of families on society can outweigh the total effort of both public education and religious institutions. Families have considerable impact on most areas of human growth and development. The interest of parents or guardians directly relates to the intellectual development and learning of children in school. Academic achievement is definitely related to parental involvement in the life of the child. Parents and siblings greatly influence the development of social competence and skills. Both mental and physical health has been tied to the family. Most certainly, the principle aspects of moral development, religious beliefs, and the concept of spirituality relate to family influence on the children. Even the economic well-being and personal happiness and satisfaction with life are related to the effectiveness of family relationships. As families go, so goes the church and the nation.

Research has demonstrated the impact of families on the intellectual development of children from birth through primary and even beyond secondary education. A powerful dynamic that can support learning is evident even at birth. Some research suggested that inborn qualities, those existing at birth but not hereditary, are acquired during fetal development. Evidence exists that some results of mother-child bonding at birth have been evident five years later. The well-bonded mother talks more to the infant during infancy and childhood and this results in higher intelligence as compared with children without satisfactory mother-child bonding experience.

The church must see the parents as the primary teachers of the children. The quality of family involvement in the growth and development of the child limits the public school system and the religious education aspects of the church. If clearly understood this could revolutionize the traditional approach to education as well as the way the church approaches the education of children. The first three years are crucial in the life of a child; the foundation for later learning depends on this period. The most effective way and least expensive way to influence children is working through the parents. Normally, parents are eager to receive information and support for their role as their children's first and most important teachers. The parent's social status, educational level or cultural and religious background makes little difference in their appreciation and receptivity to assistance with their parental roles. The nature of parenthood means that each parent wishes the best for their children. The church must be a willing companion in this process.

Educational policy or local church programming does not normally recognize the family's role in educational and religious foundations. The assumption that once children start to school that the school is the major influence is false. Families not only make a powerful impact on the way children learn but the influence of the family actually outweighs that of the school. As early as 1966, the Coleman Report funded by the U.S. Department of Health, Education and Welfare reported that schools do not overcome social and educational disadvantage. Children arrive at school unequal and leave even more unequal. Coleman found that family background, rather than the school inputs, most strongly accounts for differences in educational achievement.   Could this be true also in the realm of spiritual development? Did not God intend the father to be the priest of the family? Does the church not understand the power of motherhood?

Family interest in a child's education may actually be the most important single influence on academic progress and spiritual formation. Family concern can outweigh the problem of size of the family, parents' income or social class. Several studies have confirmed Coleman's findings, but little change has taken place in public policy. The church has taken even less notice on the value of families in the religious education of the children. It is clear that the school or the church can not overcome the neglect of children by their families.   The family cannot adequately delegate this responsibility to others, but by what authority may parents be held accountable?

Research for the past thirty years has consistently found that differences in academic achievements are more related to the family than to the quality of the schools the children attend.   Families not only affect learning achievement, they are a powerful influence on mental and physical health, social skills, economic well being and contentment.   Reported data also speaks to the negative influence of family conflict and stress.   Chronic family discord has been associated with many behavioral problems.   Notwithstanding the negative impact of bad relationships, research supports that a stable family relationship can produce great benefits for family members and the community.   This has direct bearing on the church.   What is the church doing to support the family? Is the church aware that many programs actually keep the family apart and contribute to the absence of parental influence at crucial times in the life of children?

A significant component of educational research and budget support should be given to the family aspects of education, but it is not.   It is clear that the parents should have more support and be involved more in the process. Parents should be partners with the school system and the religious institutions in preparing the next generation. Nothing significant has been done to alter the balance of power in education.   Schools neglect parents and leave them out of education except in the aspects of "negative involvement."   Since parents are contributing as least as much to learning outcomes as the teachers, one would expect that parents would have access to information, resources and training for this role. This is not the case. It is not only in the field of education that the denial of the family contribution occurs.

The church, in spite of all the talk about family values, does little to support the value of the family. Some claim a pro-life position, but do little after the birth to assist the mother or the child. One should not spout political slogans without understanding the consequents. Surely one could both oppose abortion and care for the child that is born to the unwed, poor or irresponsible parent? Where is personal integrity in this matter? What value does the church place on the unborn, the new born, and the growing needs of all children?

Concurrent with the Coleman study, some religious leaders began to search for answers related to the drop out rate of children and teens from the church. It was discovered that some local church programs were divisive to family relations and actually hindered the spiritual development of the child. Some suggested that the nursery experience be limited to diaper changing and breast-feeding so those infants could stay with the mother and experience worship. It was evident that children needed more bonding time with the family during worship and it was expected this bonding would strengthen the child's future worship response. This was totally ignored by the church.

Some inborn characteristics are present at birth but are not hereditary; they are acquired during fetal development. An individual's natural sense of the good is normally present at birth. Since learning begins in the womb, the Christian training of children should begin with the pregnancy or before. The fetus clearly responds to food the mother eats, to music, to the mood of the mother, and to the external environment in the home. Would the worship and devotional experience of the mother not also influence the fetus during the months of pregnancy? The mother-child bonding at birth and their nearness during the early years of life accelerates learning. Why then does the church not take advantage of this and program for the child to experience worship in the arms of the mother or the lap of the father?

During the past three decades, the local effort to baby sit the children and teach worship to children in a separate service has continued to develop. Now, most parents will not attend a church without these perks. Yet, this programming is detrimental to the psychological and spiritually development of the child and their identification with the family and the church. Since a child learns even in the womb and early bonding experience marks them, what must their earliest subconscious memories be of church? To be left with strangers, in a strange place, to cry for their mothers, is this really what we want for the children? What are they expected to learn in an over crowed, under staffed nursery? What do they experience? If the first impression is the most lasting, no wonder the children are ultimately lost to the church.

This is not to say that the church does not need a program to assist new families with children who have never been exposed to worship. Also, there may be cases where the needs of the parents for a period of time out weight the immediate need of the child. In such cases, a nursery or children's church program could be useful as a temporary measure. The problem is when these conveniences become a norm for all children in the church and there is little if any understanding of the true nature of what takes place. What can be the outcome of parents who willing abandon their children to the "baby sitting services of the church" so they can be free to "worship" while the child suffers the indignity of sense of abandonment?

Two examples illustrate this concern. Recently a pastor came to me with a problem. He was having difficulty with a father who insisted on bring his young daughter to the worship service. In spite of encouragement from the minister and others in the congregation to use the nursery, the father refused to leave his daughter with strangers and insisted on holding her on his lap during the worship service. The pastor and the people thought this was a tragic, selfish act by the father, when in reality it was a normal and logical act by a loving father. The father worked six days each week to cover the medical expenses of a sick wife. Sunday was the only day he had to bond with his child. The pastor's dilemma: if he insisted on the nursery -- the father would stay at home, if he did not, the congregation would complain. Has the church lost all sense of family responsibility to children and parents? Does everyone want a child free worship service? If so, what about Christianity as a family faith? Will family life affect the next generation's participation in the church?

Another case was a family that moved to another city and took a young son to visit a church. The child was taken from the parents at the front door and placed in a beginner church service with other children while the parents joined the regular worship service. On the way home the young boy said, "I don't wike it, I just don't wike it!" The child wanted to be with his parents. It was a strange place, much like the first day at kindergarten, and was an unnecessary alienation of both child and parents from the church. The father's response was "I don't wike it either!" Tragically this couple never found a church where they could personally care for their son.

As the church continues to program for each age group on various days and evenings of the week; the family is further divided. By the time a child completes elementary school and almost total alienation exists. They want, and even demand, separate church programming as teens. This seems to be good on the surface, but down deep it is a form of separation from the principle function of the church: that of bring families together and into communion with each other. As the "separate but equal" programming continues, whole generations are lost from the church. With the total secularization of public education and the faulty programming of the church, it should seem obvious, to even the causal observer, why there are so many dysfunctional families and half-filled churches. One only has to view a local congregation on any Sunday morning to understand the missing age cohorts. The children are not there. The teens are not there.   A few middle aged married folk and some older people remain, but whole generations are away.   Is this the result of programmed alienation through the years?

How could the church assist families? Where the church can assist in the development of a transcending influence on the family is in the concept of team leadership.   A team approach to ideas through church staff leadership that includes parents in the discussing and hammering out of the idea related to family programming is a winning combination. When this concept is promoted out of the cauldron of interaction, both the church and the family becomes more stable. It should be remembered that the break down of the family increases the problems in church and the community.

A starting place would be to clearly understand the qualities that constitute a strong family. When children develop well and parents function adequately as adult members of society, these families have many of the same characteristics. They are affectionate, communicating, forgiving, humorous, loving, nurturing, sensitive, sharing, spiritual, and supportive. How many families do you know with these characteristics?

It is primarily the way members relate to one another and the outside world that creates a family that builds or weakens the individuals and the unit as a whole. Qualities such as the ability to communicate, a wise use of power, a special bond of love between husband and wife, appreciation and support of each other, assists with the maintenance of their religious beliefs. It creates a respect for the spiritual values and distinguishes between families that strengthen or fail to protect their members from the forces that destroy family unity. These are non-material, relationship qualities that both one and two parent families can manifest. This, however, does not mean that the church can be ambivalent about the value of marriage.

Data does not support the contrary views of marriage. Some say marriage is good for men and bad for women and that the institution promotes inequality. Violence against women has caused some to postulate that marriage is unsafe. There is strong evidence that marriage benefits both mental and physical health. Research suggests that to be single, widowed, separated or divorced is harmful to one's health. Married individuals report more happiness than the never married. Men and women are about equally satisfied with their marriages. More violence exists in *de facto* relationships than in legal marriages. Among married people in the United States, marriage quality is the strongest predictor of overall satisfaction in life. Married individuals, as a whole, do better in almost all respects than do unmarried persons. There is less antisocial and socially disruptive behavior among those married. Where these facts reflect wise selection of well-adjusted persons or some effect of the marital situation is not known, but the church should more effectively advance the value of families. A good and stable marriage is the best foundation for both the church and society.

The willingness of the church to accept more female leadership grew more out of a lack of men than an effort to advance women. Notwithstanding the actual reasons for opening the door to women, there has developed a kind of feminization of the church. This sends the wrong signal to men, who are already in short supply. The message, although unintentional, communicates that the church can get along without men. This is no more the case than it is in the family.

When only one parent is interested in the religious matters, the children are further confused. Children often think if being a Christian were so great surely dad would be interested. In fact, believers having children by unbelieving spouses have produced a kind of "impure" generation (I Cor.7.14). This infection has grown into a social epidemic of drugs, gangs, and savage violence. The intensity of family dysfunction has changed both society and the church. The stew pot is simmering.

Some families survive without a father, but the message to the children is confused as to the role of the father. This complicates ones view of God, as the Heavenly Father. Research demonstrates that one normally attributes the same qualities to God, the Father, as are attributed to a biological father. Growing up without a father has complicated evangelism in the inner city. On one effort the literature had to be changed to place an emphasis on Jesus as the Big Brother rather than God as a Father. The church must be careful to give women a rightful role in advancing the church, but care must be taken to send the right message to the men. Men are essential to produce children and they are important to the propagation of the gospel.

Most Americans are wary of too much government intrusion into families; this gives the church an opportunity to influence the nature of the family. This has been neglected. A little effort by the church could influence better decisions by the parents, particularly about both parents working. Many poor families are stable. Other families have everything and are still dysfunctional. The church could deal more effectively with the problem of greed, materialism, and managing the family budget. Many in the church could be adequately assisted with the funds that are wasted on buildings, full-time staff which work only a few hours per week, and elaborate programs for people who do not need them. In fact many of the activities of the church actually work to divide the family unit into specific program units.

The mothers of two-thirds of America's children work outside the home. This sharp increase from a generation ago is not all related to the needs of the family budget. It is part of the lifestyle changes that have become operational in society. The percentage of working mothers has increased steadily since about 1980. There is nothing in the current programming of the church or the structure of American society that suggests these changes are temporary. The percentage of mothers working outside the home will probably increase in the future and with this phenomenon the perils for the American family will increase proportionally.

Tragically, studies find that most of the working women do so because they desire to do so. All of the woes of the family, however, can not be attributed to the working mothers. Many families in which both parents work are stable and wholesome places for children to develop. What this means for the church is that the working mothers provides the church an opportunity to minister to the children.

The church has failed in the matter of family values. There is a lack of role models and accountability for failure. The church has been unable to transcend the congregation's habitual religiosity as business and industry has failed to transcend the performing of required tasks. Disunity leads to dysfunctional. The church has failed to develop the compelling ideas that transcend the scheduled program. This leads to parents who fail to go beyond the day to day functioning of the family and bring the family members to a conceptual level of spiritual function.

How should the church go about finding such transcending ideas? The first source is individual inspiration. Effort must be made to influence the membership to buy into the ideas of morality and fairness. The transcending ideas must be intertwined in the persona of the parents and in the hearts and minds of the children, but first it must be in the leadership of the church. This is the problem. Such leadership often has an Achilles heel.

Should the church leadership or one of the parents stumble or become discredited, the ideas and ideals they espoused stumbles and often dies in the minds of the followers. It is difficult to perpetuate an idea beyond the tenure of the church leader when it is an integral part of the persona presented to others. What is the church doing to protect itself and others from the failure of leadership?

Failure of the church to take some of the responsibility for the failure in families also complicates the problem. The bitterness and alienation with the dysfunctional family is normally transferred to the church. Often people in the church take sides when a marriage is dissolved. This multiplies the problems of the two families already caught in the confusion of broken contracts, failed relationships, wounded children, and divided observers who watch, take sides, and shout advice as if they were at some sporting event. This creates wounded and scarred individuals who do not feel they can turn to the church for comfort or sanctuary.

The church purports to be a place filled with mercy and understanding, but the steaming stew pot clouds the manifestation of these virtues; consequently, the image of the House of God is tarnished. Often the most grievous wounds are received in the house of friends. It has been said that the church is the only army that shoots its wounded. Certainly the action of many creates a pessimistic atmosphere in which forgiveness is difficult. The church has neglected the opportunity to influence the nature of the family.

Although money is important to a family, poverty is not an excuse for failure in family matters. Many poor families are stable while other families with everything are dysfunctional. My family never took charity. Mother was widowed with three children in 1937 three months before Social Security would have been available to her and her children. Nevertheless, she proceeded to raise her children without the assistance of government or even family. She was fiercely independent. She would not ask or accept help from others. She depended on God. If someone wanted to assist her, it had to be done anonymously. If she knew who delivered the food or stuck money under the door, she would return it.

Lack of support for the traditional male/female marriage has become a problem for both church and society. The break down of the family increases the problems in education and the community, particularly in the area of drugs and crime. What are the attributes that demonstrate the value of families? When the head of the family accepts the priesthood of the family and assumes a sense of ministry, a commitment to serve others, a true binding of a family unit may take place in an atmosphere of faith and security. This is required to raise a family or build a church.

Leadership in the family or church is not dependent on how one earns a living; it depends on ones relationship to God and relationship to people. The adequacy of ministry is not determined by ones financial status, but by ones spiritual commitment. The effectiveness of ministry does not depend on what one starts with materially, but what one starts with spiritually. Ministry relates to being adequate to the present task. With God's enablement, men and women called to build families or churches are equipped by the Holy Spirit and enabled to utilize the competence adequate to accomplishing the task without loss or waste. It would be a great asset if the church would operate in a way to enhance the functionality of family roles.

There are at least four stages to social change. These changes are similar in the church and families. Some call it progress, others see it as advancement, but in reality it is just change. In fact, little or no progress or real change occurs; things are just repackaged. The first stage is **excitement.**   There is genuine optimism about the present and the future. The swift pace of sociological and technological change dramatically shortens the duration of enthusiasm for any endeavor be it social or spiritual.

Next is a period of **assimilation** when understanding and learning proceeds at a rapid pace. Learning wanes as excitement cools, but during the period of excitement one assimilates a great amount of data, insights and perspectives. As a sponge, one soaks up all relevant data. As excitement cools and an information overload occurs **disenchantment** interrupts the progress of assimilation.

As the flaws in people and institutions are observed, disenchantment happens. When changes and behavior do not square with past experience, disenchantment encroaches on the intellectual and spiritual development and begins to lessen the confidence of members in the organization and the people. This precipitates an empty feeling and breeds **dissatisfaction** with the *status quo*. This creates an opening for change. Members began to actively search for alternatives. This ultimately leads to **extraction**.

Unless a deliberate and timely effort at renewal takes place "negative participation" begins and extraction is not far away. Both churches and families require persistent effort and involvement to maintain agreement. Little is accomplished with limited participation.   Excitement comes only from deliberate, reflective thought and consistent effort.   In fact, no good will comes from the limited involvement of one who is already discouraged.

Both the church and the family require sustained, deliberate, reflective thought until the cycle is returned to excitement. Church and family are similar to the growing of a garden.   A garden requires diligent cultivation, careful prayerful planting, saintly patience, and adequate work from the gardener. After man has done his part, the garden must be touched by the Hand of God to be fruitful unto harvest. This is also true of marriage and family.

Congregations and families suffer from similar difficulties: poor communication, disorder, outside pressures, loveless relationships, sin, lack of forgiveness, deficient agenda, and weak commitment to the value of marriage and family.

The lesson is clear: the church and the family often fight the wrong battles. The battle for the Bible and evolution are examples of battles lost when the church permits the discussion to get to the courts.

Whether it was the Scope Trial of 1925 or the more recent California battle for scientific creation it was a no-win situation from the beginning. The theory of evolution was just that, a theory in the textbooks, until a few zealous folk attempted to force their beliefs about scientific creation on the general public. The court won and everyone else lost. Some fight nobly for prayer in the school, when the real problem is a lack of prayer in the home. Others urgently fight abortion, but neglect to fight for the adequate upbringing and education of those already born. Certainly the church and the family have legitimate concerns for the unborn, but the primary responsibility must be to the children already in the homes, or in the courts, or with grandma, or on the streets.

A meaningful lifestyle for the family must replace dependence on either public education or the church to teach morality and ethics to the next generation. Principles and values are taught better by example than by exhortation. A positive attitude must be developed about the next generation. When the church or parents begin with a negative attitude about the young, there is little hope for a positive result. Parents must reject the cathedral and the state as the primary teachers of the young and return to a kind of contemporary house church where family values can be learned in the process of valuing families.

The problem of children must not be framed within the educational or religious paradigm of the present policies. Somehow the community and the church acquired precedence over the family. Families must regain their God given priority. Children are produced in the context of the family unit. The community must protect and the church must preserve the children, but both must perform their tasks in the context of the family. Children must remain the wards of the parents. When parents are not Christian, the effort of the church must be to reach the entire family. Although scripture suggests that a child shall lead them it is not often that children with un-churched parents are able to win their parents to Christ. The worth and value of the individual, each soul, must be restored to the conscience of American Christianity. Parents, with the support of a renewed church and a re-valued educational system must wage an aggressive battle for the next generation, if Christianity is to be viable in the next century.

Families cannot expect assistance from the state. It is not the responsibility of the government to promote family values. When politicians attempt to advance such an agenda, the public sees it as a means to win elections, not real concern. In the end the preservation of wholesome families depend on the families themselves, especially on parents who set standards for themselves and their children and then enforce these standards with tough love applications and good examples. The church can help in building the men and women who become partners in creating the children. These parents must be assisted in becoming spiritual leaders in the home. The church can provide the materials and the guidance for parents to become the principal teachers of morality, most by example. During the constitutional convention, Benjamin Franklin suggested that since "God governs in the affairs of men," the delegates should begin each day by praying to God for guidance. There were various objections and Alexander Hamilton ended the discussion by declaring that he did not personally "see the necessity of calling in foreign aid." When the Constitution was completed, there was no mention of God anywhere in the body of the document. Although the right to the free exercise of religion was clear in the First Amendment, the secular foundation of the United States was clear in Article VI of the body of the Constitution. "No religious test shall ever be required as qualification in any office of public trust under the United States." Although 11 of the 13 original states in 1787 had religious tests for public office, a majority of the convention adopted the wording without debate.

This is a pluralistic society and a secular state; the family must not and cannot depend on the state to teach the principles of Christianity or to strengthen the Christian nature of the family.   There is hope that in an effort to be moral and ethical, the American society will create an atmosphere in which Christian parents, with the assistance of renewed churches, can grow and prepare the next generation for Christian involvement in the secular world. Jesus prayed, "Father, I pray not that you take them out of the world, but keep them from the evil."   It can be done, but it must be done by parents or guardians who see the value of families.

What exists now is a self-contradicting paradigm. This paradox was forced upon the American family, by a state controlled educational system that refuses to follow its own funded research about the value of families, and an over programmed church that has forgotten the simple act of faith and neglects the essence of the Christianity mission. The family must come first. The educational program and the church have a place in the development of the child, but it is not primary. The primary responsibility must be the parents and these other institutions must assist the parents with their task.

Somehow the family must find a place of focus in American society. Perhaps one should long for the time of the family room at home, the family car, the family church and the family pew where the whole family journeyed to church together and sat in a designated pew and furnished some family fire. Could the loss of that family fire be an answer to the present uncertainty or perplexity in the husband-wife, parent-child, and church-family relationship? Somehow the family must rekindle the fire at home, bring it to church and send it to school. Without such a renewal there is little hope for the American family or the American church. Somehow the church must develop a relational theology that is relevant and clear.

VI. CONGREGATIONS FAIL TO ADVOCATE RELATIONAL THEOLOGY

Churches reproduce systematic rather than relational theology.

Theology should be the study of God and His Word, but it has become the study of what many writers think and say about God and the Bible. Any effort to contextualize an application of theology to behavior has been neglected. Christianity has not established a relational theology for those who embrace the faith. Almost no effort to defend or plead for a more practical approach to the reality of theological interpretation has been made by the Christian leadership. The concept of the Incarnation should prompt theologians to make some linkage between human behavior and theology, but the persistent effort has been to organize theology systematically based on the thoughts and opinions of other generations with little if any contemporary application.

The word "theology" itself is the combination of *theos* (god) with logos (word). The idea of theology did not originate with Christians. Historically it entered the literature when the Greeks attempted to develop a synthesis of the myths of the Olympian deities with prehistoric myths. Later, theology assumed a philosophic form and became either a rational expression of myth or an abandonment of myth and identification with the metaphysics of "being." Through the impact of Greek theoretical thinking, theology entered Judaism and Christianity. Jewish tradition has resisted the idea of theology, while some cultures such as the Oriental have no concept of theology. Without an understanding of God from either the Greek or the biblical perspective, one does not readily construct a theology.

Man tried to combine biblical tradition and Greek philosophy, but it did not work. Looking over Paul's shoulder to the written words, it is almost impossible to get into his head and heart, or reproduce the circumstance and atmosphere in which the hearer received Paul's writings. The reality of the Word of God is clear: the Word was made flesh and lived among men. Since the words are presented in some abstract or historical form rather than the living language of the people, such words will not communicate the genuine message of God. Paul suggested that believers were living epistles open and read by others. Remember the New Testament era did not possess a copy of the New Testament. The people were mediums, and the medium was the message.

Some classical theologians have called for a more relevant methodology that looks ahead and moves forward. Basic Christianity has been an extension of the horizontal present moving to meet the contemporary needs of people. With the Incarnation, God intended the plan of redemption to meet the human family at the relational level of need. Christianity has always functioned in the secular historic present looking more to the present needs and future state of individuals, rather than looking back.

Historians have attempted to make the church more powerful and more influential on the affairs of state, when in reality the institution itself was not a direct influence on the state. Christianity changed individuals and these committed persons through their lifestyle and decisions moved the state. What is often lost in the large view of history is the value of the individual and the impact that one good person made on a cause. Sometimes such individuals were called martyrs, at other times simply forgotten or written off as rebels.

History gave too much credit to the institution rather than the effect of changed lives on society. By making it appear the church was doing the good rather than individuals, the wrong message was sent to the next generation. Consequently, great effort was made to build the institutional church rather than incarnate Christianity in a practical way. Those called to present God's grace to the current generation have been sidetracked in the wilderness of history trying to learn the way it worked in the past and replicate the process. This blinded them from seeing the current needs of the people and using the mind of Christ and the assistance of the Holy Spirit to minister at the point of need. Time would be better spent looking to the present needs of the people and finding creative ways of changing individual behavior. This would enable the larger groups, the family, the community, the church, and society to be more moral and ethical and to acknowledge that God intervenes in the affairs of men.

Christian Theology has been the study of religious principles, the essence of godliness, and meditation about the relations between God and the creation. Theology has been a cognitive or thinking reaction to the Word of God when individuals needed an affective or feeling response. Perhaps only the Holy Spirit can transcend the culture of the ages and adequately illuminate the scripture for contemporary minds.   Certainly there are no private interpretations of scripture, but the Spirit does make direct application of spiritual truth to the hearts and lives of individual believers. Somehow an atmosphere conducive to the objective reading of scripture must be created with the aid of the Spirit, which would permit sincere believers to view the Word without the gross interference of the academics. Perhaps then the Word could work effectively in the heart. Anything less simply adds to the dilemma.

Biblical theology is a segment of Christian theology that attempts to set forth the knowledge of God and the divine life by hermeneutic procedures of the Bible as a whole, and not by isolated passages. The science of hermeneutics is to determine the meanings of words and phrases in context, and interpret it to others; it is sometimes called exegesis or reading the internal meaning out of the scripture as opposed to reading into the scripture external implications. Biblical theology is a discourse about God based entirely on the content of the Bible. Even with this lofty goal, it is not free from the prejudices of the individual interpreter or the influence of culture.

Systematic theology is a constructive method that strives toward a complete, philosophic, and a systematic statement of the comprehensive content of theological knowledge as interpreted by previous academics. It is a discussion "about" God based on the compiled information from all past writings on the subject. It includes both the bias of selection and elaboration. Biblical theology is not less bias, which is part of the problem. The Bible, as well as the words, thoughts, and opinions of others about the Bible, are selected and expounded upon based on a personal orientation or sectarian prospective of the interpreter, at times seeming to violate all logic and relativity. This is why each individual believer should seek the guidance of the Spirit as the Bible is read and studied.

Academic scholarship requires that any organized and methodical study of theology present the facts and permit the reader to make a judgment about the meaning and value of information. This is not so in any division of theology. A theological treatise is often a position paper slanted to defend the author's sectarian position.   In other words, it is not an effort to inform or interpret, but an attempt to persuade another to a particular point of view.

Through the years, this approach to biblical explanation and doctrinal interpretation has become a kind of freeze frame theology: ideas, concepts, and representations from the past are lifted and presented to support a present position.

The theology of Paul did not assume a systematic form; it was more relational. Most of the theological constructs of Paul had little chance of being understood until the changes initiated by the Reformation transpired. Even then it was interpreted in the light of existing culture and presented as if it were fully understood. The effect of culture is not clearly understood and this affects the interpretation. Some doubt the Bible can be understood apart from the culture in which it was first given, but surely there is a way through the maze. The Bible means exactly what it meant to the first person who heard it. How can we then understand?

Over time, the concept of Biblical theology has fallen into disfavor because of sectarian interpretation of scripture. The alternative, however, although more systematic and less biased, is still flawed by the freeze frame problem and personal bias of selection and interpretation. Perhaps a different approach to theology could combine the better of the two methods through a simple relational view of scripture rather than the complicated historical hermeneutic perspective.

The concept of a freeze frame theology comes from the trend in systematic theology to duplicate the writings of a previous time and place in an attempt to use it without the appropriate consideration of relevance to the present generation. The writings and teachings of past spiritual leaders are not only reproduced; they have often become a kind of religious or sacred counterfeit. At times these reproductions suffer from limited understanding of the original discourse. The result is a product that the early spiritual fathers would not recognize as a valid issue. Generally, there is no effort to deceive by this process; it is more of a forced effort to authenticate the present argument. Somehow in religion, the older the references the more legitimate support it lends to ones argument. It has to do something with "first evidence" or something.

It is true that one must respect the past and appreciate the foundation upon which present academics stand; however, duplication of the philosophical ideas and theological constructs of the past can lead one down the path of fallacy. This difficulty is caused in part because most systematic theologians have not developed the ability to deframe. It appears easy to reframe the words of others, but difficult to deframe one's own perspective.

Deframing is a term that suggests the ability to shed one's past frame of reference together with a willingness to adopt new ones that are more appropriate under prevailing circumstances. The truth is clear: the past does not always adequately inform the present. However, when one becomes emotionally attached to ideas and constructs that have come through both education and experience it becomes increasingly harder to change.

Religious convictions of the past deteriorate even during the generation in which the constructs were produced and often utterly fail to be relevant to the next generation. A New Testament example of this comes from Peter's attempt to put past Jewish traditions on Gentile converts of Paul. A free translation of Paul's reaction could read, "As Paul grabbed the chin whiskers of Peter, he shook his finger in Peter's face and said, "Why put a burden on them that you and your fathers could not bear?" When one attempts to impose a spiritual frame of reference that is not relevant to a current situation, great injury can come to the cause of Christ as innocent people fall through the cracks of current ambiguity.

How does deframing work? When one faces the first signs of failure, the normal tendency is to work harder to make the existing frame of reference work. Churches for generations have been working harder and longer to make disciples, but to no advantage. A frame of reference change, or deframing, equal to the altering of the Christian perspective from Peter, the Apostle to the Jews to the focus of Paul, the Apostle to the Gentiles, is required for Christian understanding to advance. Keep in mind that the change did not come easy for Peter. He resisted God, his companions, the circumstances, and ultimately himself to keep the old frame of reference in tact. One certain thing in life is change; however, change in the church has been viewed as dissent or heresy. The repercussion for religious leaders who nourish change has been devastating personally and professionally.

A difficulty in deframing is contained in the way one perceives information. Current frames of reference are used not only as regulation about action, but as a paradigm to comprehend what is seen, heard or felt about the situation. When one encounters information that threatens the current frame, it must be considered immediately or change can never take place. Such threatening information is usually dealt with by either ignoring it or questioning its validity or by attacking the motives of those suggesting change. Often the resistance is subtle even subliminal and usually nonverbal. When one consciously attacks a new frame of reference, at least the difference has been considered and the new idea has a chance of eventually being accepted as amended by current understanding.

The most perplexing part of deframing is that one must do two things at once. The old frame of reference must be used as a basis for decision-making while accepting new information that may temporarily discredit ones current position. This requires a willingness to examine the uncomfortable information objectively and dictates that one put the data outside the present frame of reference for appraisal. The Bible states that the way of man seems right in his own eyes. The truth is that no one ever clearly sees themselves from the perspective of others; consequently, the wise leader will assume that everything is not clearly seen and will listen and learn from others. When things are not working, one must be willing to consider the alternatives. This is difficult and probability explains why no significant change has taken place in Christianity in the past four generations.

Scripture deals with being connected to God, to family, to friends, to enemies, and even being connected to causes. Relative terms are used to infer relationships such as master and slave, husband and wife, father and child, neighbor, enemy, and the list goes on and on. Even the evils of immorality are presented in relational terms. Adultery was seen from the perspective of violation of the marriage contract by adding another to the relationship. With other opposition, fornication and the sin of keeping company with a harlot were classified as evil because of the absence of a lifetime commitment. Both good and bad in scripture are viewed from a relational perspective. Sex, for example, in an uncommitted relationship is sinful, but in the context of a long-term commitment it is sacred.

Relatives are connected by marriage contract or blood. A blood relative is a person related by birth. Individuals who have the same gene pool are kinfolk and are a part of ones larger or extended family. The Bible deals with both the connection by contract in marriage and the relationship by birth. The meaning of the Virgin Birth, the purpose of the Incarnation, and the nature of physical death in the Crucifixion of Christ were elements of the divine plan or atonement to be blood related. In reality "blessing" literally means: blood related.

The intention of the Virgin Birth was veiled for generations. Before knowledge that the father supplied blood to the fetus, the idea of a virgin birth had little value. From a faulty perspective of the absence of human sexual intercourse, it was used to explain the sinless nature of Jesus. In the early history of man, the thought that a female could conceive without the assistance of a human male was incomprehensible. Once the true nature of paternity was understood, there was a logical explanation for Jesus, the Messiah, being the only begotten Son of God.

Jesus was related to the lineage of David through Mary and to God the Father through conception. Although the ways of God are past finding out, an understanding of paternity made the divine intention of Incarnation more understandable. The purpose of God in the birth of Jesus was to build a bridge of relationship to the human family. This was to be done by using Abraham to build a family through which the Messiah could enter the human family as the kinsman redeemer. Christian believers were to be related to Jesus by adoption into the Family of God.

When divine acceptance occurs, individual believers see themselves as joint heirs with Jesus Christ in the eternal kingdom of God.

Scripture claimed the Incarnation was eternal: the eternal state of Christ was to be that of a man. There is one mediator between God and man, the man Christ Jesus. Upon His return to Heaven, Christ told his disciples He would petition the Father to send another Comforter to be an ever present Advocate for them on the human journey. Was this not a continuation of a relational demeanor?

Relationship is primarily one of blood. The crucifixion process caused the shedding of blood, but that was not the cause of death. Crucifixion was death by suffocation. As the body was weakened by a loss of blood, the legs could no longer push the body up to enable breathing. When this weakness occurred, the victim died of suffocation. On the occasion of the Crucifixion of Christ, Roman Soldiers were impatient for the victims to die; therefore, the soldiers proceeded to break the legs of the thieves to speed the process. Breaking the legs of Jesus was unnecessary because of the volunteer nature of His sacrifice. Scripture explained that no one would take His life that it would be given up voluntarily. The kinsman redeemer had already commended His spirit to the Father so there was no need for the soldiers to break His legs. Greater love has no man than the expression of giving ones life for relational perspective?

Study of scripture today lacks the energy and perspective of the first generation believers. The first believing disciples were personally acquainted with Jesus. In fact they were selected and called to be learners at the feet of

Christ. Many in the early church also knew the spiritual leaders of the movement. They knew Peter, James, and John. They knew Barnabas, John Mark, and Luke. When Paul journeyed to Rome he knew the names of at least twenty-one friends. These friends came to visit him while he was under house arrest in Rome. Paul did not preach in the arena. There were no big churches on the corner with advertised and scheduled services. The ministry of Paul was restricted to teaching only those who came personally to visit with him. Paul's letters are filled with personal references about his companions, his enemies, his colleagues and his concern for individual Christians that were scattered around the Roman World. When the Bible is read from a relational perspective, it has a human face; consequently, the ancient writings are more compassionate and benevolent and have more relevance to present human problems in society.

The Bible uses words filled with relational meanings. It is a book about relationships. One sees personalities of the biblical world interact with one another and the record clearly shows both positive and negative aspects of the relationship. For example, the Old Testament dealt with the sins and conflicts of spiritual leaders such as David and Solomon. The New Testament clearly showed the confrontation between Peter and Paul and the conflict between Barnabas and Paul. In his letters to certain churches, Paul even identified the troublemakers.

The Bible is filled with information about friends and families.   It speaks of kinsmen, sisters, brothers, parents, companions, and the company of believers, husbands, wives, and children. It speaks of fellowship, communion, sharing, participating, loving, knowing, and understanding.   All the relationship words are there. What if one could be freed from sectarian views or the systematic recorded thoughts from the past and clearly view the panorama of scripture from the perspective of functional relationships?

The Creator is presented in the Holy Scripture as a God expressed in three Identities.   Why one God would be manifested in three personalities unless mankind was expected to relate to each disposition: God the Father, Jesus the Son, and the Person of the Holy Spirit?   The Supreme Being anticipated that mankind would build a relationship with each of these particular personality roles and consequently be more personally and literally related to Divinity.

Each of the divine roles is to relate directly to a particular need of the human family. Since God revealed Himself in terminology that man could comprehend, obviously each Identity is to have a function in the life of a Christian. The Father is related to the forgiveness of past sins and the Believer's present position in the Family of God. The Son brings safety, security and the level of intimate friendship to the relationship. The Spirit provides the ever-present assurance and support for a believer's lifestyle, witness and Christian service in the everyday world.

God the Father is the Forgiver. He, for Christ's sake, forgives sins never again to be remembered against an individual. It is through this forgiveness that one is accepted into the family of God as a child. Although an individual is accepted as a child with the rights and privileges of a family member, most individuals perceive themselves as a servant of God rather than a child of God. Childhood is a stage of formation in both the family of man and the family of God. St. Paul described the state of childhood (Galatians 4).

When one receives a birthright as a child, the heir is owner of the whole estate but is little more than a servant. During childhood, the heir is under control of guardians and trustees until maturity prescribed by the father is reached. Normally, one does not realize the significant aspects of relationship until maturity. During the growing process, elders are both understanding and forgiving and treat the heir as a child not a servant. As the child matures, a greater knowledge and a fuller understanding of the father are reached. It is the same in the spiritual family.

Jesus is presented as the Son who is Savior. To be saved is to be safe. It is Christ who provides the security and the sense of belonging to the family. Identification with Christ and understanding one's relationship with Him is the first mark of spiritual maturity. As one develops a friendship with Christ, the understanding of Father God increases and one gains spiritual knowledge that is essential to walking daily with Christ. Jesus told the disciples that to know and do the commandments of God was to be in a friendship relationship with Christ. As the disciples matured, Jesus told them, "I do not speak of you any more as my servants; a servant is one who does not understand what his master is about. Whereas, I have made known to you all that my Father has told me; and so I have called you my friends." Moving from servanthood to friendship brings one into a level of intimacy with Christ that produces great knowledge, joy and security.   With this level of intimacy, one can journey forth as a witnessing emissary for Christ.

God the Holy Spirit is presented as the *Paraclete,* one called along side to bring aid, comfort and support to Believers. The Holy Spirit is understood also to be the intercessor and advocate to plead one's case and to protect one in the midst of spiritual warfare. The ministry of the Spirit primarily relates to the Christian witness as a life in contrast with contemporaries. The Spirit is the Enabler for both the Christian life and Christian service.

In a systematic theology, the function of the Godhead has been lost in the Doctrine of the Trinity. The emphasis was on three members being one Deity rather than seeing the Supreme Being expressed in three Persons. A relational view of the Trinity would be more realistic and applicable to the contemporary requirements of modern humanity. The relational view would provide more understanding of the character of the Godhead, more attachment to the nature of Deity, more connection with the function of spiritual leadership, more devotion to the role of the divine, and a greater bond to the integrity of the Christian message.

Through a relational view, the Godhead has more resemblance with the human family and a greater association with the understood roles of life. Seeing Jesus as the elder Brother changes the whole picture of spiritual relationships. Realizing that believers share in the Family of God and are considered joint heirs with Christ of the eternal kingdom certainly brings a realistic understanding of anticipated rewards prepared for the faithful. One must remember that the pristine church of bible days did not have a book called the New Testament. They possessed an understanding of a new covenant relationship with God and other followers of Christ. They saw each other as an open book to be read as witness to the transforming grace of God and the meaning of fellowship in Christ. No individual member of the group possessed a copy of the New Testament; it was not yet written.

Scripture records only one lay person possessing any of the Old Testament. The Treasurer of Ethiopia, who had the wealth and station to go up to Jerusalem, purchased the scroll of Isaiah. He did not have the entire Jewish Bible, only one book. It is true that he needed someone to explain the book because it was from another culture. This is an isolated case of Philip, the deacon from Jerusalem, explaining to the inquirer about Jesus from the writings of Isaiah. In no other biblical case is a portion of scripture used in the conversion process. In fact, the opposite is true. The conversations were related to personal knowledge and experience.

The lifestyle witness of individuals brought Christ to individuals in the early Christian church. Paul told others to "Follow me, as I follow Christ." He also proclaimed that his life was an open book read by others. As the world observed Paul and other early Christians, they saw the living word of God in action. The impact of this witness was later recorded for others to read for encouragement. The Bible was written to believers in the church about believers who had made the journey in the First Century. The New Testament was the written record of a process and described the relationship between good and evil in the interaction of people. This has relevance for today!

Teaching scripture alone does not bring individuals to Christ. Scripture may be used as a tool, but most often it is the observation of the Christian lifestyle and the kind word of a believing friend, together with the work of the Spirit, that brings individuals into the Christian faith. In the early church there were no academic arguments about the meaning of words, only a sincere need to understand the teachings of Jesus Christ. As the letters and books were written that later were gathered as the canon of scripture, there were no long disputations over the meaning of the message. The language was common and clear.

The words were read once to an assembled group then passed on to others who did the same. There were no reasons to stop and explain the use of words; the writing was within the family. It was as if one were reading a letter to a blind brother from their father. Both the writer and the receiver understood the language in the context of the culture. The words came from friends, persons known and understood, dealing with real issues related to the lives of those present. One thing became clear, others could not teach the Christian way of life; it must be caught through personal contact with another person. It was relational, passed on to family and friends and freely received as good news.

Christ came to bring a ministry of reconciliation to the world. The purpose was to reconcile man to God and man to man; that is, establish friendly relations. Reconciliation requires movement or change on both sides of a relationship problem. Sin had separated man from God. The Incarnation was movement on God's part. Men only had to accept the reconciling work of Christ to establish fellowship with God. This process teaches mankind the procedure for mending bad relationships on the human level. It seems that it takes two to make a contract, but the action of one can break the agreement of the parties. God has made a covenant with man: accept Christ and become a part of the Family of God. The Church was to be an instrument of God's grace, caring for believers and their families as the redemptive process went forward.

Tragically the church became something else and those who wish to follow Christ are misguided and confused by the signposts they see on every corner. How many ways are there to Heaven? Christ is the Way, the Truth, and the Life, and all men must come to God through Him. The message is lost somewhere in the midst of busy activities and hurried lifestyles. Each succeeding generation becomes less and less Christian. Unless drastic action is taken to reconcile man to God, there is great tragedy in store for the Christian hope as well as the American dream.

Christianity is a way of life, not a theological scheme with which one must be in total intellectual accord. An essential element of Christianity is loving Christ and one another. When the clear message of Jesus is so loaded with creeds, ceremonies, and teachings of others; a first century Christian would not recognize it. All this, together with church squabbles and an exhibited intolerance for the point of view of others, has made the basic message fall on deaf ears. Christianity is a love relationship with Christ, not the teachings of others about Christ. Since all truth is of God, Christianity must accept all truth even if it is stated in a manner that offends their intellectual sensibilities.

Every denomination contains some valuable truth, but none contains all the truth. Each sees a part of the whole picture, but no one is able to rise high enough above personal culture to see the whole picture. Each approaches the sacred in their own way out of their own cultural perspective. One approaches God in silence, another in music, and others through some rite such as baptism. One may want incense and liturgy, others personal experience or fellowship in the midst of worship, but they all seek God. Honest people hold irreconcilable different beliefs about Christ, but they all claim to be Christian.

It is as the Armed Forces of the United States: the Army, Navy, Marines, Air Force, and Coast Guard; although the joint actions of these forces demonstrate differences, all are loyal to the U. S. Constitution. The various branches of the military have different functions with the ultimate goal of protection of life and liberty of the American people and preservation of the Constitutional Government freely elected by the people. Why can't Christian groups who claim the same goals and the same Lord work together to spread the gospel?

Christ never demanded belief in some particular theological position as a prerequisite to discipleship. He asked individuals from various walks of life to become His disciples. They were learners and had to grow in understanding and acceptance of the details.   Christ called them to friendship with Him. From the early days of primitive Christianity, believers professed their faith in some form of a creed or quasi-creed affirmation. This was not to test the correctness of individual doctrinal beliefs as much as it was a pledge of loyalty and an expression of firm confidence in God.

Testing orthodoxy by creeds was a secondary function that came into being during the fourth and fifth century. Some considered the process a necessary evil and to others it was a millstone about the neck of believers making it difficult to lift their heads to see the future. No doctrinal argument or theological construct equals the common sense insight of basic faith in God. With faith, all else essential comes to the believer. The early followers of Christ certainly did not walk together in total harmony; neither did they have uniformity in the procedure of sharing and receiving the gospel.

There are assorted theologies in America; Barth, Tillich, or Niebuhr influenced most of the prevailing streams. One could make a case, however, for a strong influence by Dietrich Bonhoeffer over a younger group of theological thinkers. Bonhoeffer was executed April 9, 1945 by the Gestapo, just seven days before his camp was liberated and one month before the end of the European war. During the two years that Bonhoeffer prepared to die at age thirty-nine, his letters from prison to friends have had a decisive theological influence on some religious thinkers. Bonhoeffer's fragmentary works have made a meaningful impact, although Germany and Switzerland, the traditional intellectual sources of Protestant theology, chose to ignore Bonhoeffer. Two years of preparing to die in the midst of man's inhumanity to man made him a visionary for the end of the century.

Bonhoeffer was able to look beyond traditional theological views and see a more practical aspect of Christianity.

His view of ethics and discipleship touched the heart of men caught in the secular age. He witnessed misplaced faith in the state and the loss of theological influence by the church. He saw the ideology of the state eclipse the theology of the church. The fanatical commitment of Germany to the philosophy of the state was a direct outcome of failure by the church.

In prison, without the structure of organized religious services, Bonhoeffer was forced into a primitive view of Christianity and the basic functionality of the individual believer. He discovered that God was not the direct answer to every question or the immediate solution for each problem. The limitation of his confinement liberated his mind and soul. He began to think as Paul must have thought in jail. Bonhoeffer witnessed the end of a theologically structured age where the church had great influence. He observed first hand the inexcusable behavior of men who professed to be Christian. If this were the outcome of the past generation's teachings, then the church required some drastic thinking to change course.

In the most intriguing concepts related to ethics, discipleship and the secular society, Bonhoeffer saw that the years of teaching by the church had almost no impact on a German soldier's conduct. His own confinement required a personal discipleship experience of meditating alone and learning at the feet of Jesus without the intervention of the organized church. As the national soul of Germany grew into a blasphemous force and became a sacrilegious instrument of evil, Bonhoeffer had a premonition of the decline of organized religion and the rise of a godless secular state.

Bonhoeffer spoke of a world with an accelerated pace toward secularization, of the powerlessness of religion in such a world, and the increasing lack of relevance of religious leaders and organized religion. Although misunderstood by some, his seminal ideas are more relevant today that they were when written in a German prison cell. Why do his ideas have influence? The world Bonhoeffer saw in the dim vision of a death cell has become a reality. Separation of Church and State has become the separation of God and state. As the world becomes increasingly a secular society, religion seems powerless to impact morality and ethics, and clergy and the organized church have lost the ear and attention of the populace. The mind or the secular souls of the masses may be looking elsewhere for answers and solutions.

As churches prepare to reach the next generation, Bonhoeffer's concepts seem more relevant. He dealt with ethics, discipleship, the secular society, the loss of religious power to influence significant events of the day, loss of credibility of Christian leaders, and the waning influence of churches. Realistically, Bonhoeffer did not see these things as bad of themselves, but as instruments of God to force individual Christians to develop a lifestyle that did not depend on organized church activities.

Renewal is possible. The circumstance of the present church is nothing to be compared with the birth of Christianity. The Faith did not begin in a religious vacuum. Mankind was not found wanting for something to believe. The new Faith had to fight against entrenched religious beliefs that had existed for centuries. Most of the religious beliefs had degenerated into feeble superstitions and meaningless rituals; others seemed to be new and vigorous.   The ancient condition almost describes the present condition of American Christianity.

The beliefs of pagan society bred superstition and fear. Moral decay was unbelievable.   The world lived in the shadow of physical death from disease and war.   During this time, light was as darkness and the corrupting forces of evil worked beneath the surface of world order. Animism, state and emperor worship, mysticism and magic, together with the occult, joined the dark thoughts of man's philosophy and the dim twilight of Judaism to prepare the world stage for the birth of Christianity.

To be relevant in the Twenty-first Century, the church must embrace a God who empowers man to do things for himself. The work of creation is finished. The work of Christ in saving the world was completed at the crucifixion. Christ sent His disciples into the world to do greater works than He accomplished. Christ prayed the Father to send the Holy Spirit to enable believers to act, to walk along side, to encourage and defend, to empower each one for the journey, alone if necessary, into the secular world of humanism and abject secularization.

Christianity was to be a lifestyle, not a cloistered ghetto afraid to venture outside the four walls of the church. The saints were to become the caregivers, the problem-solvers, and not the state.   Bonhoeffer claimed there were no problems that only God could solve, following the empowerment of the individual believer. Certainly there are problems, but God must not be petitioned to meet every need of the human family. A man, who does not work to support the family, the church, and even provide taxes for the state, is worse than an infidel. And infidelity takes many forms.

An infidel is different from a heretic. Heresies come from the ability to choose for ones self. Anyone who does not hold to what another considers an orthodox position may be considered a heretic in the eyes of some. In reality, three hundred Protestant CHURCHES come from the same source. When one holds a doctrine or creed that is contrary to another that is heresy to some. In such case, is one denomination correct and the other 299 filled with heresy? Surely, not! We must find a way to work together to reach the present generation.

An infidel is something else altogether. People who want God or the State to do everything, fits the concept of infidel. To understand a person who does not carry a proportionate and appropriate share of the support burden for others, one must look at several entities: the atheist, deist, freethinker, skeptic, and the unbeliever. An atheist denies the being of God. The deist believes in one God or a divine providence, but rejects revelation. A freethinker rejects the tenets and traditions of formal religion as incompatible with reason. The skeptic is one whose faith in the reliability of evidence is weakened or destroyed, so that he/she doubts religious teachings. An unbeliever is one who does not accept any religious belief.

Have you met any people that match these definitions? The secular society and carnal church are filled with just such people: people who have varying degrees of faith. People who want God and/or the government to do all the work will not accept responsibility for their own actions or accept the obligation of support for others. How does this fit into the idea of infidelity? For the most part, the definitions are labels for excuses for not participating in religious or community functions. These various expressions of infidelity are part of the humanistic and secular society that feels uncomfortable in a self-sacrificing role of a laborer. The unfinished work of Christ, the work He left and assigned to believers, will never be accomplished without a new and transforming work of God's grace that transforms both the motives and the direction of life.

The established church, which is often a meeting of "saints who have not been caught", may call this heresy because it is at a variance with generally accepted theology. Obviously, the present theological constructs and patterns of religious practices have failed to rally the people to follow Christ. Perhaps America does need some radical theology based on contemporaneous action that is relevant to the Twenty-first Century instead of the continuing effort to preserve the past.

America needs a theology of action that is militant enough to mobilize the scattered groups of believers into a mighty army of sharing saints. Provided the various Protestant groups could forget their dissimilarity and focus on sharing the good news and developing a fresh comradeship within a stable company of believers, renewal is possible.

Jesus chose twelve men to be His companions. These men had a special bond of affection; in fact, the inner circle was given nicknames: Simon was viewed as a kind of foundation stone, so Jesus called him the "rock man." James and John together were boisterous and loud so they were called the sons of thunder. These were just the kind of men to build the future church. The naming act suggested a friendship that would develop and grow. Jesus did not make intellectual demands on these early followers. Most interesting about this early band of disciples were various backgrounds and points of view? The early learners accomplished a great deal by putting aside personal differences and concentrating on obeying Christ's commands. These men changed the world without a written creed or elaborate structure. These followers of Christ had no permanent buildings, organized activities, or social agenda, yet they became a force for good.

The basis for membership in the early group was friendship and a willingness to put aside one's personal agenda and commit to full obedience to the commission of Christ. The basic truth that unites must be greater than individual differences. To love one another has greater power than being orthodox, because love has the strength to accept differences. Love can enable strangers, even enemies, to work together for a common cause. When that cause is the good news of Jesus, the love of God is extended to those outside the circle. This can and must be done in the marketplace, not within the four walls of a church. Why would a confessed sinner, who does not yet trust Christ, want to be with those who are frustrated and angry about the way the gospel is presented? To present the glorious news of the gospel in such a dull, boring, and meaningless manner to those who venture searching for a way out of their personal dilemma, is both a shame and a tragedy. Dull services using archaic, ambiguous words, are making even the faithful search elsewhere for fulfillment. Why then would one expect a stranger to seek moral or emotional strength in the confusion of a scheduled church service?

The church is losing thoughtful and sincere people from the membership ranks, because they do not feel at home in the churches due to language used or the doctrine taught. They must exercise mental reservations or make private interpretations that would make them intellectually dishonest; therefore, it is less painful just to stop attending the church services. How long can the church stand imprisoned in worn-out concepts and theological constructs imported from another age? The spirit of Christ has almost irresistible magnetic pull on the faithful, but they continue to drop out of active participation in organized activities. This does not mean they have abandoned their basic faith. To the contrary, it may mean they prefer to go directly to God without the hassle of the "group thing."

Although there can be no direct comparison between the field of medicine and religion, both are concerned about the welfare of people. If medicine still used the old wives tales, snake oil, bleeding procedure and many other practices endorsed by the medical profession 100 or 200 years ago, no one would seek the aid of a Physician. Tragically, when the public feels that the church is using outdated practices and holding to old constructs, passed down from other cultures and other counties, no wonder many do not seek assistance of the clergy. The big question: why do religious leaders hold so tightly to the words, phrases, and theological constructs passed down from a bygone era?   It has to do with things old being better, but if the data is not relevant to the present generation it will not benefit either the church or the people.

The church is so deeply committed to a set of technical propositions that they alienate rather than attract people they actually seek to serve. The value of the gospel story is not the theological constructs of the Virgin Birth, the Resurrection, or the Return of Christ; it has to do with the character of Jesus Himself and His relevance to the current generation and to the present social setting.

There was a time when the church depended on mystery, a kind of secret, but now words and their meaning have value to the people. The church cannot forever continue singing and preaching to the choir. There may have been a time when liturgy and a sense of blind faith in the system were enough to breed loyalty of the congregation; that time has passed. The Word of God has been translated into the vernacular of the people and they want to know the meaning of the words used to express the teachings based on the bible. Most, if not all, efforts to explain to the satisfaction of the people fail. Although there is no private interpretation of the scripture, there is personal feeling about the value for one's life. The systematic theologians convinced the church that people must have a cognitive approach to the scripture, when in reality it is mostly affective. What they feel is usually more important that what they intellectually comprehend.

Seminaries, where the basic work on theology is done, have become less important in recent years. It seems that seminary type students are more interested in marketplace action than the bland study of works from previous generations. The social issues have gripped men and women who are concerned about ministry. Seminaries in the past have been incapable of innovative action in the social arena. A few new ministries have taken on a Para-church character and are providing the intellect and the action-based leadership to initiate creative ways of reaching and ministering to the disenfranchised.

These popular approaches are changing the means of communication for theological ideas. Publishing has moved from textbooks to journals, paperbacks, and electronic journalism. It is difficult to sort through the mass of material and this may be a good thing; it could force honest believers to think for themselves and seek the guidance of the Holy Spirit. Perhaps a closer relationship to the expressed Persons of the Godhead would build a confidence base upon which the church could proceed. The pragmatic obvious is clear: the younger generations of Christian leaders are doing the work of the ministry rather than just reading books and arguing with others about the past. In spite of institutionalized religion, a few committed Christians are doing the work of reconciliation that brings redemption to mankind. Provided church leaders embrace basic principles as their own, and such movement does not develop into another denomination as all previous efforts, there is hope! Hopefully, the new effort will be based on common principles compatible with basic biblical truth that was the under girding culture of the early church.

VII. CONGREGATIONS FAIL TO AVOW CHRISTIAN CULTURE

Churches develop civil rather than Christian culture.

Pristine Christianity developed the elements of a common culture that served as an umbrella simultaneously for most subcultures. Individuals accepting Christianity changed some lifestyle and practices, but not all. The converts remained and functioned within their native culture, but identified with the larger community of the saints. Christianity did not begin within a single culture or ethnic group, but brought people together into a common life from a wide diversity of races, cultures and other religious backgrounds. Early churches started in houses and involved whole families. Christianity, as an organized religion expressed in the local churches of today, owes much in its history to many others than the professional elite. Many made significant contributions to the cause: scholars, writers, artists, architects and historians. There were both saints and scientists, philosophers with ideas, men of action, and a few secular leaders. The professional leadership was shaped both by their culture and by the nature of their behavior.

The ordained ministry was defined while the church was still a persecuted minority, long before the church entered partnership with organized society. Christian ministers were not born to the role. Each future leader was born an amateur, some outside the influence of Christianity. Conversion and a call were necessary to open the door to leadership. Despite the different names used by different congregations: clergy, priest, presbyter, minister, pastor, all professional leadership performs the same functions. Inside their church they possess authority; a superior or a democratic process may limit it. Nevertheless, they maintain authority to perform rites of the church and to exercise influence in certain spheres within the church and sometimes the community at large.

When institutions are powerful, the structure normally becomes deaf to criticism, and when institutions are weak, designated leadership is usually unable to act upon even constructive criticism. The church as a social institution is neither as powerful nor as weak as some critics have suggested. Those who see the collapse of organized religion may be irritated because the fall does not happen immediately. It is similar to the "death of God" theology of the past when some critics asked, "If God is dead, it is sure taking the clergy a long time to bury the cause and probate the estate." In fact, the leadership of CHURCHES is immersed in the moral, ethical, legal, social, and economic aspects of the institutions. Many aspects of life are bound up in the institutions and cannot be simply wiped out of existence. Whether the criticism concerns ineffectiveness, authority, or elitism little can be done in one generation to make significant change. This is part of the problem.

The entrenchment of institutions causes them to persist long after their usefulness is over. Tradition and custom are as hard to break as a bad habit. With the clergy continually propping up organized religion, the function of the local congregation may become less a spiritual force, and more of a civil or moral conscience to society. The ability to influence is not all bad. What is bad is to lose the basic cultural atmosphere that made the church Christian in the first place.

Current Christianity has developed a kind of ecclesiastical hypochondria. This is a state of depression and anxiety regarding the spiritual health of the church and the many imaginary illnesses suffered by local congregations and individual members. In fact, many local congregations developaphilosophythatcommunicatestothemembership that the institution missed something when they were not present rather than a more positive attitude that the individual missed something by not participating.

The fact of negative participation by most of the membership in the past has not affected the program of the church. Past discussion concerning the declining influence of the church has been fruitless. The futility of the facts seems to depress church leadership and efforts to force participation does not work. Most would rather look to politics, global warming, world famine, or the rash of terrorism directed toward Americans, than deal with the real problems facing the local church.

Christianity has become the only part of organized religion that measures religious performance by the regularity of attendance at weekly services. This evaluation of attendance is primarily an American phenomenon. No other religion has attempted to manipulate followers in this manner. Public contempt for the church also results from this effort. The record shows an alarming decline in active participation in scheduled activities, if not the spiritual life, of the church. This negative participation will not produce a positive outcome for organized religion.

The decline in weekly participation in religious activities is apparent. The lack of converts, the vanishing budget, the public disclosure of clergy immorality, all contribute to a public contempt for the church. Not only are there declining numbers in most aspects of the local church, the church has been unable to maintain even the existing proportion of the increasing population. Children of church leaders, families of the faithful and even the poor who historically have gladly listened to the regular proclamation of the good news, are no longer present or have turned a deaf ear to the message. Frequently the poor look to other institutions of secular society to provide for pressing needs. Efforts to increase funding for basic human needs, such as food and shelter have faltered. The pattern is not the same in all CHURCHES or communities, but the trend exists and is malignant.

Self-serving explanations have camouflaged the trend toward decline. Some disguise declining participation with renovation projects, new locations and new buildings; others explain loss in terms of a migrating population or changing communities. Some claim the membership has settled to a "despised few" because of the emphasis on quality rather than quantity. Despite the method of concealment or the change in appurtenances of the church, the influence on America by Christianity has declined. Many events sponsored by the church have taken on a civil or community identity rather than being a religious ceremony or event.

The clearest evidence of decline in church participation is in larger cities, particularly the inner-city areas. Whether they abandoned the poor or whether the poor abandoned the church is not clear. Those who were previously eager to participate in the life of the church now depend on drugs, sex and gangs to provide either excitement or a sense of family. The rich and famous, who rarely depend on the church, continue to ignore religious institutions unless it has some political or bottom-line value to their career. The community church is no longer a primary source of family cohesiveness or support. Yet, the church provides many services to the community: baptism, weddings, and funerals, special holiday observances and opportunities to celebrate special family anniversaries. Many of these are participated in out of tradition rather than religious fervor. The quantity of the special event participation creates a false sense of life in the church. Although the special events such as baptism, weddings, funerals, Easter and Christmas are important, they alone do not clearly represent the practical aspects of the Christian way of life.

There are both social and political aspects to religious protocol. The participants, more from a civil perspective, may view a particular religious ceremony simply as a community event. Notwithstanding the failure to see the events as religious, the event actually performs a social role and becomes a stabilizing force in society. Some do not see religion as a part of their personal life, but they see religion playing a social role, dignifying and making an event acceptable or traditional. Those who see or use religion in this manner do not feel a need personally to belong or participate in the regularly scheduled religious activities of a local congregation. Actually, the church and state work together on many such issues which causes the role of the church in the community to be further diminished.

There are advantages in stable marriages. Christianity developed religious insight into the meaning of the marriage relationship and made the married status of a woman that of a person instead of a link between a man and his children. The laws that regulate marriage and the ceremonies that solemnize them are a social necessity; they are required to protect all parties and particularly the women and children. The state and the church, for the moment, agree that a partnership of one man and one woman should endure and be a haven for both partners and the children. The nature of the ceremony and the legal papers filed with the court confirm this agreement.

When a minister performs marriage in a church, it cannot be called a relic of the past; however, in the present secular society, the process is more civil than Christian. The behavior is more that of an adversary than an adherent. The request for a church wedding is more out of tradition than as an act of religion; it is not necessarily participation in the spiritual life of the local church. These outsiders, although not true adherents, want to behave in a manner appropriate for church members, but without the personal commitment. They want to bring up their children under the influence of the church without making the dedication as a faithful member. When this is permitted, the process becomes more civil and traditional than Christian.

Baptism is another ceremony that brings the family together and stresses personal responsibility of individuals. In some religious groups, water baptism is public acknowledgment that the individual has accepted the Christian faith. In other cultures and religious groups, baptism is related to the naming of the child and becomes a kind of religious counterpart to the legal registration of the birth.   Regardless, the event brings a sense of responsibility to the family, together with those who witness the event.

The funeral service and the burial provide benefits for both the family and the community. The ceremony of transition and the hope the process instills in life beyond the grave is a stabilizing force for all concerned and a legally regulated disposition of the body.   For families who express no interest in religious services, the funeral and other special services are viewed as little more than a civil event.

In countries where religion has less influence, the state must provide for marriage, birth records, and disposition of the dead. The tragedy here is that many in America participate in the ceremonies related to birth, marriage and death without a commitment to the religious institution providing the service. It is as if the process is seen as some necessary event mandated by society. Whether one leaves God out of the process or rules God out of the various passages of life, in reality, there is little difference. It seems in the areas where the church provides the most service to the community; the religious values are neglected or not understood.

There are other events in life where one encounters the overlap of religion and society. In court, one may place a hand on the Bible and swear or affirm to tell the whole truth. The U.S. Senate or the Supreme Court opening with prayer by a chaplain speaks to the issue. In addition, the military chaplaincy with its ministry of presence recognizes the need for religion in the life and activities of society. Memorial services for the dead of wars or terrorism manifest the need for religion in the life of the population. When a survey showed that 2,400 sailors were members of the Islamic faith, the U.S. Navy appointed its first Muslim chaplain. This officer became the second Islamic chaplain in the military; the U.S. Army had already commissioned an Islamic chaplain.

These two appointments demonstrate the lengths even the government will go to provide an indication of order and care for the religious and cultural needs of groups. When the state participates in such decisions, a large body of literature regulates both the process and the participation. Those who receive the services provided by governmental authorities often see the events as civil rather than religious. Little, if any, advantage is gained by the religious institution. The separation of church and state is so complete in the minds of some, the events are considered civil rather than religious.

Although the church still has some influence in America, the institutional church has been unable to bring sufficient strength to the family unit to make a difference. The breakdown of families and the dissolution of marriage are not significantly different between church members and the public. Spiritual leaders have not affected the social problems or general morality than community leaders. The church has had no significant impact on sexuality in America. In earlier generations, the church could distinguish between fertility and sexuality. Clergy and parents could inspire personal responsibility in the young together with respect for the procreative powers. Yet, the church has been unable to formalize a process to affirm chastity before marriage or fidelity in a monogamous relationship.

Primitive societies celebrated the beginning of adulthood and honored fertility as the source of life. Some religions are uninhibited in relating sex and religion.   Christianity is conspicuously silent about puberty and the beginnings of sexual activity.   Although Christianity celebrates the marriage relationship between one man and one woman, the emphasis is on the legality of the commitment rather than their relationship. The church has said little about the sexual union. The New Testament advised husbands to follow the example of Christ's love for His Church. This became the model for husband-wife relationship. It was not sexual, but was loving, caring, and ultimately intimate.

Sexual responses were to be the logical out growth of a close and intimate relationship and procreation the predetermined outcome. Some see the "one flesh" idea as the consummation of marriage when in reality it is an expression of the results of the physical union: the child. Husband and wife are not kin to one another and the sex act does not make them one person. It is the sharing of the gene pool that produces a child designed to bring a couple into an even closer bond. By misunderstanding the "one flesh" statement, the Biblical concept of "knowing" which constitutes an essential ingredient of intimacy is lost in the process.

The doctrine of original sin, unknown in the Old Testament or the Gospels, came into Christianity by the writing of St. Paul and was elaborated upon by St. Augustine. This teaching hindered the development of a Christian understanding of human sexuality. The sex act was barely redeemed by its procreative powers and then only in the marriage relationship. Christianity has never adequately come to terms with the passion of sexual love and consequently the dawn of sexual awakening is never celebrated as a gift of a loving Creator. These facts have caused Christian leaders to overlook, neglect, and utterly fail to teach male-female relationship in the context of scriptural knowledge and intimacy. Civil law has defined prohibited sexual contact as "carnal knowledge," but the church has failed to teach adequately the intimate relationship that prepares a couple for the responsibility of sexual activity based on a relationship of spiritual knowledge.

The New Testament itself does not adequately inform sexuality; it deals with right and wrong relationships. One must look to Genesis to find the remote premise: God created male and female. For Christianity to place the intimacy of relationship between male and female on such a high plain, as knowing one in an intimate way without the ultimate expression of sexual love, was to confuse the people and confound religious leaders. It seems that the divine concept of sexual love was to grow out of a loving relationship of mutual consideration for one another and an adequate regard for the procreative power of the act. Without long-term commitment to one another and ultimately to children and grandchildren, the physical act of sexual love is misused and abused. The concept of platonic love, amorous even sensual, but purely spiritual relationship, is considered an impossibility in modern society. It is, however, exactly the intended foundation for marriage. This foundation is obvious: the ability to relate to one another in a wholesome manner and remain sexually pure until the ultimate commitment of marriage. It is the long-term commitment that sanctifies sexual expression.

Although Christianity has neglected the physical aspects of a marriage relationship, those religions and cultures which have placed emphasis on sexuality have not been the ones that have uplifted women. The female's fertility, not her sexuality, ought to be the object of adoration. Unable adequately to express the respect for fertility, the church has abandoned the process and left the celebration of both romantic and sexual love to the imagination of secular society.

American society deals with romantic and sexual expression through many instruments of modern media. Many of these are brought directly into the home by way of the television and the Internet. Free speech has even protected the Internet and made volumes of sexually explicit data available to young and old alike. Secular society cannot get beyond the sexual conquest or triumph over sexual appetite long enough to achieve a meaningful relationship. In fact, the process has degenerated into a perpetual adolescence that is implicit in the failure to take responsibility for the procreative power of sexual expression. There has been no maturation in this aspect of the man-woman connection since the dawn of recorded human history.   Part of the problem is that modern America cannot see the relationship between reality and language.

A structural relationship exists between language and reality. The means depends not only on the structure of the words, but differentiation made about the words and the variability of the definition and use of words in relationship to the organization of the communication. An event or a fact occurs but once, and the meaning does not stay the same over time. Reality has a process character, while language has a structural base. This is one reason the church cannot give the essence of religious ceremonies to civil authorities.

There is a fundamental difference between the structure of the language and the structure of reality.   This lack of sameness makes communication difficult and is particularly true in the social and religious arena.   The reality is that there are more things spoken of than there are words to express them; consequently, words are chosen to explain the reality from the perspective of one person or one group. When the church fails to communicate a moral position, then society will establish the parameters of behavior.

The relationship between language and reality must be understood both to comprehend the failure of the church to deal with the sexual issue and the progressive debauchery in society. The worsening change in society is due in part to a change in the meaning of words and the structure of the English language. Without such understanding, the delicate connection is strained and words create a fabrication of fantasy and delusion. The free use of four-letter words and sexually explicit language is part of the problem.

Humans, in a purely verbal form, retain a great deal of information and the meaning changes over time. First hand experience is the basis for language structure. Eventually the interlocking of definitions and reality, words are used in relationship with other words and a statement is tied to observable facts or personal experience. Humans normally interpret words in the light of themselves. They often hear what they want to hear. Both the eye and the ear may be gates to the soul. One must also understand that a great deal of communication is not words but is sensed through nonverbal means. When others add words and meanings to a nonverbal message, the meaning is expanded. This is part of the problem with language as it relates to religion and morality.

Misunderstandings and disagreements arise because the same word is used to refer to many different things. Not only may the same word be used to refer to different things, but different words are used to refer to the same thing. Individuals see things from different perspectives and use different words to describe what they see. Therefore, both the scripture and the courts require more than one witness to establish a point. The church can only influence moral actions when the behavior of Christians becomes worthy examples for others to follow. The state cannot decree morality. Neither can the church extract moral behavior from an immoral soul. The church cannot by dogma alone effect change in human behavior. Christianity has always demanded a personal commitment to change and a forsaking of old ways of thinking.

One current problem with language in America is that the language is English. The English language contains many thousands of words and many of these have more than one recognized dictionary meaning, yet English is far from having one word for each fact. Many words must do multiple duties and represent a variety of facts. The communication problem is due to the structural differences between language and reality. The semantics of English suggest that it is primarily a two-valued system and seldom more than three valued. The facts are either yes or no, up or down, north or south. The culture or the language seldom allows for middle ground or a third option. The effort to see both sides of a question often fails because there are many more sides. This makes the middle of the road policy or one of moderation a difficult road to travel in social or religious issues. Normally, they require an either/or extreme rather than a middle course or another alternative.

In American politics, a Third Party does not have a strong appeal because of the either/or choice the people make. The choice between two is hard enough to make; a third choice available creates an almost impossible process. Americans often see success or failure with degrees between not mentioned. A political party could lose a national election by one percent and the press would consider them a total failure. Part of this is the limited capacity of the common language. The social issues such as race, poverty, welfare, or abortion are normally an either/or issue choice. Those who seek moderation or a third alternative are normally branded negatively by both sides.

In religion, people are separated between Jew and Gentile, Catholic or Protestant, traditional or nontraditional. There is little acceptance for those between. This is exactly the problem with Christianity in America: one Lord, one faith, one baptism, has become 300 CHURCHES each of which seem to exclude the others.

A positive choice clearly infers a negative attitude toward the others. If one chooses to be a Baptist, it suggests a rejection of the other 299. The exclusiveness is a form of either/or choice and is caused partly by the structure of the English language and culture. Reality consists of degrees of political, religious, or social feelings.   It is never just black or white, good or bad, democrat or republican; there is always more to the story even if it goes unexpressed, but it is difficult for Americans to understand and accept this middle ground.

Language is a distinctively human characteristic. Since it was learned as a child, it is naturally reflexive; consequently, most never come fully to understand their own speech or that of others. Many communicate orally and few learn the art of written composition. When most Americans write, it is usually talking on paper rather than thinking on paper. Americans just talk and often do not know what they have said after they have spoken. There are more facts than there are words to refer to the facts. Most people can express their ideas or concepts orally better than they can in writing. This is part of the problem. Preachers say one thing; theologians write another. The effort to communicate what is written in the Bible or the work of Christian scholars is often distorted by the pulpit interpretation of the words.

When philosophy, theology or government policy is written down, most people never read the manuscript. The meaning comes from some commentary or spin on the written word. Americans seldom read the fine print of insurance policies or other contractual arrangements. Lawyers are hired to do the reading. Often presidential candidates do not even read the precise wording of a political platform on which they are expected to run. They simply do personal commentary and political spin work on the issue without regard to the written words. Much of the Congressional Record is never read by even those who passed it into law or those who comment about what the record says. Often the excuse for not giving precise answers to a question is stated in terms that one has not read the document or comment about which they were just talking.

Writing has advantages over speaking. Writing increases the awareness of language; it is more specific and is less likely to be forgotten. Writing is less likely to be misunderstood than speech. Primitive societies managed to maintain their culture and lifestyle without a written language, but to achieve advanced society writing and other methods of making permanent records were required. That schools have not taught Johnny to read and the clear evidence that most adults gain their facts from listening or watching rather than reading for themselves, are serious issues both in politics and religion.

Many human problems tend to arise out of the nature and structure of language. Problems are characterized in language and solutions are sought and written in the same language. Failure to deal adequately with social, political, and religious differences actually stems from a misguided persistence to understand a many-sided, many-valued reality by means of a language limited primarily to a two or three valued structure.

Reality is process while language is more static. People and the world change more rapidly than language changes. Words change over time because words are defined in relation to the thing or event described. As the same word is used to describe new things, the meaning gradually changes. This is why dictionaries are revised occasionally. Old people normally complain that the young people have no respect for the mother tongue. Translating words, thoughts, and literary constructs from another language or culture, the meaning of words change, whether it is the writing of Shakespeare, the words of the King James version of the Bible, or other classic works of literature, the meaning of words are changed over time though linguistic innovation.

Classical scholars of past generations would be shocked to see the strange vocabulary that has evolved. Past scholars would also be concerned about the strange interpretation given to some of their writings. The theological and political truth is that linguistic innovation actually changes the meaning of what was written. The Constitution of the United States is a good example of a modern court interpreting the words of the founding fathers in situations and under circumstances that the authors could never have anticipated or even imagined.

The problem is greater than just a political agenda, the language itself has changed over time and the original intent of the author is lost somewhere in the process. The whole culture has changed and language is just one expression of the cultural change. A clear example comes from the New Testament. Classical scholars translating the King James Version (Titus 2:14) selected the word "peculiar" to describe the redeemed.   In 1611 the concept of peculiar came from Roman law, meant "private property", and described the special place Christians had as the "private property of Christ." The word now describes people who are odd, strange, or funny looking. The term is no longer a badge of honor as a Christian, but has become a word of rejection and exclusion from the mainstream of society. Such circumstance is part of the problem.

When one is forced to view reality through the medium of language, they blur the picture at best. In fact, the reality of the past does not exist today. The words used to describe the reality of a Century ago have lost or changed their meaning. The structure of language is more rigid than the process of reality. Summer camps for young people used to schedule a commitment service around a campfire. It was called a Faggot Service because of the bundle of sticks given to the participants. As young people cast a stick on the fire, each was encouraged to give up bad habits that would hinder the Christian witness. Since the word is now used in a different context, can one imagine the church sponsoring such an event today?

The reality of today is different from the reality of yesterday, and words are less adequate to describe either the reality of the past or the reality of today. This further complicates the understanding of writings from the past, especially when they are expected to be understood enough to affect present society. Yet, that is exactly what the church expects. Accepting the past does not adequately inform the present.

Some years ago I was speaking to a community church in the Baltimore area. The subject dealt with living the Christian life, a life of separation, committed to a holy walk, etc. As each point was made an elderly gentleman stood in the back and declared in a loud voice, "Call him John, brother, call him John!" I was dumbfounded. Finally, after several interruptions, in the final review of the sermon, I said, "In days past, some would call what I have been preaching: sanctification." At that "word," the old man jumped to his feet and said, "That's right brother, if his name is John, call him John!" This individual could not accept definitions of the word, new descriptive terms or contemporary operational definitions; he wanted the old word: "sanctification." The new terms had no reality for his understanding.

Where does the church get reality and how does one characterize it sufficiently to write down the present experience and remain true to religious traditions of the past? There are no easy answers, only intelligent choices. It is a no-win situation for most local congregations. Traditions are varied and difficult to integrate with modern needs and understanding of the population. Churches must rise above the limits of local culture and place the constructs of Christianity in a broader more universal culture in which all believers can function.

The abortion issue in American politics is an example of both the conflict of language and the conflict of moral and ethical philosophy. Not everything that is immoral can be outlawed in a civilized society; neither can one accept that everything legal is morally right. Both sides seem to want and either/or decision from the people when language and culture do not permit such a distinction. Each side can easily set up a no-win situation for the other side. The partial birth question has been a no-win issue for both sides of the abortion issue. The life or health of the mother, the issue of rape and incest create a middle ground that blurs the either/or issue. Three 1996 cases in England are additional examples of the confusion of an either/or issue. These cases suggest there are no easy, dogmatic answers that can satisfy the ideologues on both sides of the abortion issue or any of the religious or cultural issues that face a pluralistic society.

The first case was a mother pregnant with twins who decided she could only raise one of the babies. Was the choice to abort one of the twins an abuse of the right to abortion? The second case was a woman pregnant with octuplets that the doctors said was a threat to the mother's life. Would the pro-lifers insist that she carry all babies to full term? Would the pro-choice side suggest that she pick and choose? Would she choose based on sex, the least healthy? Would she abort one, three, five, seven or all? Who can decide? The third case was the issue of more than 3,000 fertilized eggs that had been in cold storage for the legal limit of five years. British law required that such in vitro fertilized eggs not be kept longer without the consent of the donors of the eggs and the sperm that fertilized them. Would a destruction of the eggs be considered mass murder of innocent children? What is the moral decision here? Who could make the choice? In the either/or issues of life, most are compelled to search for alternatives, middle ground that could be considered both moral and ethical and hopefully legal as well.

The Christian church, by dogma, tradition, sermon, and pontificating on the issue created the difficulty. Reality for most people is clear on some aspects of the issue and blurred on others. Is there a difference in destroying 3,000 fertilized eggs, abortion 1 twin or 1, 3, 5, 7 or even 8 of the octuplets (all eight died before or during delivery)? Most Americans do not feel that they should decide for another. Some suggests that only the mother could make the choice. Others say the state must control the issue. This is a no win issue in American politics. It is a controversial issue in the Christian church. It is an ever-present social issue in each community and in most families. The decision to let others decide weakens the core of religious beliefs and the moral and ethical standards of society. The same is true of many other issues on which both the church and the state take positions. This is one reason that Christianity is not working well in America.

Politicians and clergy are weak surrogate proclaimers for the morality and ethical stands on social issues. Most Americans put both politicians and clergy at the lowest level of professional credibility. The people should be speaking out about issues that affect their lives and families. Even scripture warned that the "letter of the law kills, but the spirit of the law gives life." America must call a truce on the social, moral issues that plague society and the politicians, and the clergy both put their own houses in order. Unless this is done, there is little hope of finding workable solutions for a pluralistic society.

Drastic differences in the ethnic and religious background of a pluralistic society hinder the necessary networking of ideas and the webbing of human resources to find acceptable solutions to the sickness which plagues American society. There is hope, but little probability of a cooperative effort in time to save the current situation. The big question is clear: can organized religion be restored to a worthy place in American society? A corollary question begs an answer: can the American government of the people, by the people, and for the people become restored to the point that excesses can be eliminated and the value of government be appreciated? Unless the Christian church reclaims its place of influence in the lives of the people, the outcome is doubtful.

The local church cannot reclaim a place of influence in American society unless a more practical theology is developed. This theology should be relational concerning the functional roles of modern life. Such a relational theology must also be devotional in nature and useable by new believers without the assistance or interpretation of scholars. This is the confusing aspect of present theology: multiple voices, but none seem to agree on exactly what is said or meant. This utterly confuses the people it is supposed to edify in the faith. Such a relational theology must bring practical meaning to the relevant needs of the people and not be stated in ancient jargon of past intellectuals.

Life is essentially dialogue; no one can live or die alone. A fundamental fact in human conduct is that every action is motivated by some factor. Spiritual nature is the chief possession of mankind, and when this nature is stimulated to constructive conduct individuals are motivated by a master passion. The Christian way of life is the positive virtue flowing out of the regenerate core of the heart. It produces more than mere abstinence from evil; it issues in love, kindness, compassion, and good works humbly done. The church cannot fulfill its task without believers whose changed lives are consecrated to practical Christian living. The church must have a core membership that will be active witnesses for the Christian cause. To accomplish this mission, the church must reproduce a theology that deals with functional roles and practical living in a pluralistic society.

It should be remembered that the meaning of language is in people not in words. Unless the people and their cultural orientation are understood, one can never communicate adequately with words. It is time for a practical demonstration of Christian commitment; time to build people who will demonstrate the Faith. People are saying, "We are sick of words; show us!"

VIII. CONGREGATIONS FAIL TO AFFIRM PEOPLE

Churches build buildings rather than people.

Sameness in buildings has replaced the common aspects of faith. Buildings have become the most static part of religion, especially, in a society characterized by mobility. Large investment of funds in single use property has become the greatest detriment to the progress of Christianity in America. Deserted church buildings point to a former presence and departure of a constituency. These buildings send a message of paradise lost and breed contempt for the Christian Faith. The message of faith must be established in people, not property. The objective ought to be confidently assisting individuals in establishing positive structures for relationships, but the effort to construct buildings continues.

Just as great mounds cover temples of antiquity, negative aspects of population change have rescinded the sacred trust and brought sacrilege to religious buildings. This reproach has been going on all over the world for all of recorded history. Yet, church hierarchy continues to pour scarce resources into property and buildings rather than people. The facts demonstrate that funds expended on facilities have not necessarily advanced the Christian cause. Life also adequately demonstrates that a small amount of personal attention can make a great difference in whether or not ones personal witness has value to others.

The New Testament is clear: God used people to advance Christianity, not buildings. In fact, the message is evident as to a programmed obsolescence of the Jewish Temple with the renting of the Veil between the people and the Holy Place at the death of Christ. God opened access to the Holy Place to common folk. Ways to do the same must be considered by local congregations. The church must again become the place of people; a place where the poor may hear the good news in relevant terms to their circumstance. How can the homeless trust the church when all the funds are allocated to property and staff and the poor neglected?

The migrating Israelites could pack up the tabernacle and move it with them. The Muslim can take his prayer mat along. The Buddhist can make his shrine in his room. Christians on the other hand have become dependent on a building and a clergy-led worship to maintain their active participation in the Faith. Regardless of advantages against weather and ability to shut the world out, the buildings of Christianity have become a liability to the overall mission.

Christianity, like Judaism, has been a faith of community that required people to gather together for worship. In America this aspect of Christianity has opened the door for unorthodox and fraudulent preachers on television and others going door to door to adulterate and prostitute the message of grace. This confuses the weak and baffles the public. Often ones absence from scheduled meetings stimulates a negative response by the group. As one elderly woman declared after missing a service, "The church visitors meant well, but they made me feel like I stole a horse." How can such negativity coming from a dependence on one's presence in a building be beneficial to the Christian cause? Since one can never reach a positive conclusion beginning with a negative premise, Christianity must find a better way to deal with the absence or "away" difficulty.

Although Christianity was preached in rural Galilee, the church flourished in the cities, spreading from Jerusalem to Rome along the trade routes from one city to another. The poor heard the message gladly. These were the migrants, slaves, craftsmen, and traveling merchants. The early converts to Christianity were not dependent on the land. They were often uprooted people, wandering masses without permanent homes. Even Christ claimed to be one without a place to lay his head. The advancement of Christianity did not depend on buildings; it was dependent on people sharing an active faith.

Buildings provide clues to the identity of the people who worship in them. Buildings encroach on the nature of the church as a group of individuals sent to a community to share a witness of their faith. The building becomes a silent message to the community and often invalidates the witness of the congregation. One does not need to be an architect or even a believer to recognize a mosque, a temple, a Catholic Church or a Protestant church. In fact, one can usually identify the denomination by the architecture. Baptist churches look different than

Methodist churches. Anglican and Lutheran edifices may be similar on the outside, but they are different on the inside. A Presbyterian Church is normally architecturally different than a Baptist building. The shape, age, and the symbols that decorate the buildings usually identify the denomination to which it belongs. Church buildings are recognized because they are part of the cultural inheritance of a country or community. Even when they are new, certain traditions enable one to recognize a familiarity and associate it with a particular form of worship.

The problem of new wine in old bottles is evident in the Protestant church. The cultural mix of America creates a confluence of cultures, and buildings often send mixed signals. Unlike most of the rest of the world, America has a tradition of congregations outgrowing the building or, because of the changing cultural and ethnic mix in the community, the flock relocates. In such cases, a new congregation often from a different group purchases the building and opens a place of worship. The new congregation often has religious tradition that differs from the previous occupants of the building. When the stately and traditional building has a new or radically different format for worship, the community is confused.

The mobility of America since World War II has created a migration and cultural/religious mixture not known before. City dwellers have moved to the suburbs. Rural people have moved to the city. Refugees from foreign wars settling in various parts of the country not normally impacted by immigrants have changed the face of religion in America.   A mosque here, a temple there, a new congregation in an old line denominational church, or a downtown church building being used for an entirely new purpose, must indeed confuse the image of the church.

One wonders how confused the traveling public would be if the Holiday Inn suddenly became a Red Roof Inn or Days Inn unexpectedly became the Knights Inn. Since this would be confusing in the franchised hospitality industry, changing names on places of worship would most certainly be confusing to the religious community. For example, the auditorium in Nashville, Tennessee which housed the Grand Ole Opry for many years was formerly a church. In Atlanta, a Baptist tabernacle was converted into a music center for "The Blues." At the time of this change, the message to the community must have been mixed for a time.

A church building is far more than a place to visit or gather as a group. It speaks volumes about the people who worshipped there, living and dead. Religious buildings are the icons shaped from a particular community. People shaped the buildings, by religious tradition; the structure itself represents the religious heritage of a community. To disregard this fact, is to ignore history. Look at outbreaks of Jewish persecution; such acts of violence normally began with an attack on a synagogue that represented the Jewish community. The burning of a Black Church in the South is an attack on a community, not just a building. When these communities change and others use the facilities, the message to the community is modified.

Since buildings express the essence of a religion, they create a style. This style is created not only through the work of architects, but also through the people who worship in the building. The style of a place of worship is as closely related to the heart of a particular religion as domestic architecture is to a way of life in a particular climate. The style determines the shape, size of the building and how it is entered and how the congregation uses it.

The power of a tradition to develop the appropriate visual expression underlies the influence of religious buildings. A minaret attached to a Moslem mosque is a signal to call the people to prayer. The belfry is a watchtower embodying the aspiration that its name implies. Towers of old churches send a message of security to the community. There seems to be two main ways of looking at religious buildings: some are mainly shrines from the past preserved for the sightseer, while others are regular meeting places for worship by the community. People visit a shrine occasionally, but do not attend it regularly. Only a faithful few belong and attempt to maintain the past. There is a different attribution given to a shrine than to a building that houses a regular congregation.

The existence of a special day, such as Sunday in Christianity, or religious or holy days on the calendar requires a corporate approach to religion. This leads to the habit of attending, reading and expounding scripture publicly at scheduled times. Some churches may be both a shrine and a place of worship where the habit of occasional visiting and personal devotion at an altar or before a sacred object takes place in the same building as corporate worship. To most Protestants, the church as a shrine or site to visit only occasionally is offensive. Yet, many Protestant church buildings are named as memorials to revered individuals and consequently create the character of a shrine.   Could this be why many have developed the habit of only occasionally visiting the church rather than belonging to it and maintaining a consistent participation in the program provided for the family?

Most English and European parish churches date from the Middle Ages or later. Sunday mass was the scheduled service and there were only a few seats around the walls. Many parts of the buildings were used for activities other than worship.   The church was often the only covered place in the community for people to gather. Given these facts, it is a phenomenon of the Protestant Reformation that the church became a place for some to gather on Sunday and other special days. The Christian church had survived for centuries without these services.

The forerunner of the Sunday morning and evening services did not come to England until Tudor times. The times (11 am and 6:30 PM) and length of services were printed in the Book of Common Prayer in 1549. Following this publication, attendance at the stated services became the norm for evaluating church participation. The difference of culture and people, notwithstanding, much of church tradition in the United States comes from England and Europe. The American church adopted the same basis for worship times and the same standard for evaluation: participation on Sunday.

The Reformers emphasized a change in the internal organization and use of church buildings. One phenomenon of the Reformation was the progressive removal of picture, images, stained glass, candles, fonts and other past traditional aids to worship. The less churches resembled places of worship from the past, the more exclusively they were used for worship alone. The emphasis was on authority of the Bible and consequently the regular exposition of Scripture. Preaching became prominent and the process of sitting and listening to sermons became the norm. Reformers favored the singing of hymns, first the psalms and gradually new hymns. When the building was considered part of a shrine, people visited, gossiped, but as congregations gathered for worship the perception of a shrine was diminished. The debate over whether the church should be "everybody's place" or just for the faithful few continues in both the architecture and program of the American church.

Anglican and Lutheran reformers made fewer changes in existing buildings. Lutherans concentrated on the pulpit and Anglicans on moving the altar to make provision for the audible reading of Scripture. Internal changes, with little change in architecture, by these groups made them more acceptable to historical catholic traditions of Europe.

Reformers were rebelling against the unified structure produced by the Catholic tradition, but they too seemed to seek unity, even uniformity. Calvin's Institutes, Luther's German Bible and catechism and Cranmer's prayer book all sought to preserve the Reformation through unity. Since the state seeks stability and unity within its borders, it was logical that the state in some geographical areas stepped in to assist in the formalizing of this unity. The idea of choice for different forms of worship was lost in a variety of buildings that best suited their heritage and culture.

Minorities developed among the population who felt that the Reformers had gone far enough. Some were convinced that adult baptism was the better rite of entry into the church. Such groups began to stress the church as a group from among the population held together by common faith and practice. The key was that this bond of togetherness was to be under the authority of Scripture and not the state, a monarch, or a religious hierarchy.

As an unprotected minority, such groups could not build so they met in houses and baptized in rivers. As Congregationalists, Quakers and Baptists gained tolerance, different style religious buildings were constructed as meeting houses and chapels. These different buildings could not be used as shrines. The simplicity of the early buildings with their graveyards reflected the principles of the people: in life and death they were a community separated out from the population. In life and death they were bound together by a covenant with God and one another.

As these groups became affluent, they began to build more classical style buildings but maintained the oblong or square room-like form with large windows. Later they came up with a rationale for the use of colored glass to make pictures for the windows. As the buildings changed, so the people and their worship changed.

Following the Industrial Revolution, called the red brick period in England, Methodism emerged and became active builders. As the separatist idea grew, Methodists multiplied; consequently, they built buildings, split and built more buildings. As preachers became popular they built larger buildings. Gradually the excitement waned and the crowds became smaller. The building, first built as a base for missionary type outreach, became the church field. Outreach and missions became secondary. The primary effort was to maintain the appearance of progress and religiosity. Most all activities took place within the walls of the church.

The building of churches continued but they were not filled and the poor outside were neglected. The process had come full circle. When what could be done with buildings reached an end, some took to the streets and slums to reach the poor. They used empty buildings as operation centers and mobilized the Salvation Army to minister on the city streets. Perhaps this "active sheep" structure is what the contemporary church needs.

Early American churches used available materials, mostly wood, to construct their houses of worship with a graceful spire and made it the nearest equivalent of a parish church for the local population. It was a place where family and friends gathered. The colonial style of building combined the room-shaped interior of the English puritans who wanted to purify the church from elaborate ceremonies and forms, but they went full circle and stipulated extremely strict personal behavior of members which created an exclusivity that eliminated all but the pure in heart.

As the American population moved west, some older CHURCHES were slow to respond to the needs of the people. This left the door open to the Methodists and Baptists as well as some new American groups to take advantage of the opportunity to gain new congregations. The idea of church state separation opened the possibility of equal access to the people. Those groups who went with the migration along the frontier gained strength and prominence in the newly settled areas. The people function and available material influenced the buildings.

The pattern of early migration of national and ethic groups from Europe is still reflected in American church buildings. Buildings were shaped by communities, heritage, and culture of the settlers. The embellished grandeur of European cathedrals as well as the austere simplicity of religious orders has influenced small churches and church buildings in America. Regardless of the background of the people, forms of worship and serviceable use of space shaped religious buildings. The fastest growing groups, such as the Pentecostal churches and community based groups have built modern buildings and are attracting people of communities who seek to be free from past religious traditions. Such congregations often down play their denominational identity with a more generic approach to worship and programming.

Christianity has more buildings than other religious movements. Whether this phenomenon was the result of climate, culture, or the assumption that the primary form of the church was the community is not clearly understood. Regardless of the reason for the central role of the building, the decline of attendance and the lack of outreach zeal within the United States raise concerns about the dependence on style of architecture and the functional use of the space provided by the buildings. Have buildings become a barrier to the mission of the

church? Have buildings outlived their usefulness for the
Christian movement?

As Christianity deserted the "as you go" strategy of the
first century, generations substituted a weak call to
come to the church. For generations the common life
of Christianity has been associated with buildings. The
common message has even been expressed through the
erected edifice. It appears that some believe Christianity
cannot survive without the shelter of facilities.   Others
have concluded that inviting prospective converts to the
building has not worked effectively. Still others wish to
mount a campaign that disperses active members into
society to utilize personal contacts one on one and in
small groups. Where this strategy has been tried, it has
worked well. The church must make constructive change
to reach the current generation. It can be argued that
integrating Christians into society, participating in the
work place, leisure activities, and public service could
make the difference in a growing rather than a stagnant
congregation.

History has adequate evidence of individuals and
populations who have been persecuted and prohibited
from building churches, but have survived and even
thrived. Faith can continue at the individual and family
level. Was it an accident of history that high officials
of the defunct USSR returned to the church as soon as
the Soviet Union was dissolved? One high official in the
Foreign Office of the USSR was baptized the same day the
Union was legally eliminated.   What does this say about
the function of history and the viability of basic Christian
convictions even when maintained in a covert manner?

Since Christianity is a community of faith, it appears to need buildings to maintain both the local effort and linkage with distant gatherings for mutual exchange and support. Most Christians view their faith as connectional and desire to be associated with others of similar faith. Should one compare the cost of maintaining a facility base for the church with that of other educational and social action entities, the costs would be about the same? The issue is not cost or the need for buildings; it is the function of the buildings. They must become a base of operation and cease being a field of operation. A long-term strategy must be considered that projects the advancement of the Christian cause into the Twenty-first Century. Will there be new requirements? Does the concept of mission need to be reworked? Could the church utilize the family and the individual more in the overall plan for advancement?

Since it is most probable that the church could not be deframed, one must speculate as to the function and use of present buildings as well as evaluate the commitment to expansion and new buildings. Church leadership must look to past problems that have not been resolved with the present structure. An adequate mobilization of constituency could lessen the dependency on facilities as a field of operation and use it more as a training center base. Church leadership must also evaluate the present and future needs of communicating the good news to the general public. What can be done differently? What can be done better? What can be done new? Answers to these questions could prioritize the restructuring of programs and facilities. What is needed is an honest and pragmatic allocation of resources.

In the church, the problem is numbers; the number of buildings and the number of worshipers. The church seems to have too many of one and not enough of the other. A primary problem for Christianity in America is the sheer number of church buildings and the fact that many of them are in the wrong place. Many church buildings are located on "donated land" on a back street or on the backside of some city desert. As populations moved and cities grew in other directions, many church buildings have become alone in an undeveloped part of the city. Others, at the crossroads of a community, have been bypassed by new highway or mall construction. Still others have been made redundant by the organization of new congregations of other CHURCHES. When numbers are counted and divided among practicing Christians in the community, the buildings on any given Sunday are relatively empty. A church is never half-full; it is always seen as half-empty. With declining attendance and half-empty churches, the image of an effective church is lost.

Layers of church bureaucracy have caused significant decline in the past generation. For example, the United Methodist Church has lost about three million members since 1960. The Episcopal Church has dropped about one million members and the Presbyterian Church (USA) and the Disciples of Christ have seen drastic decline during the past generation. It seems that members and money have trickled down to other sources of spiritual fulfillment, while mainline churches are being ignored.

Perhaps denominationalism is over. Current college students do not express preferences and seem to be the most un-churched group of active brains to enter academia. This means that intellectual strength that for generations supported the church will be concentrated elsewhere. The structure of CHURCHES and changing sociological patterns of America both contribute to the decline in mainline church attendance. The era of mainline Protestantism could be slipping away while bureaucrats argue about things such as program flexibility for the local church.

As the structure of bureaucracy increased, flexibility of the local program was lost and people began to lose interest in the mission of the church in society. The church was too busy running programs to attract the present generation or to maintain the interest of their parents. The age cohort 18-30 are absent from churches. When church structure and program become rigid, personal needs and spiritual concerns of the people are neglected. The concerns of the membership were overlooked because out of traditional faithfulness some continued to attend, but with mental and emotional reservations as to the relevance of the church in society. Busy activity replaced quiet devotion. Budgets replaced the process of volunteer tithing. Paid staff became surrogate soldiers in what once was a Mighty Army of volunteers, while the energy and resources of the people were squandered on entertainment and selfish activities.

Alienation from the church began following World War II. While individuals remained interested in religion and even spirituality, most lost interest in the scheduled activities of the church. Denominational identity and doctrine became less significant for some and lost meaning for others. A kind of exploratory membership became the norm. Large numbers of individuals and families began attending churches different than the traditional church of their childhood. Not only the church suffered, but other institutions also felt the destabilizing effect of abandoned moral and ethical practices and loss of principles and values in Western society. Young people began having difficulty committing to political parties, or even to the corporate structure of American business.

The entrepreneurial spirit is alive and working in America. The American way has always moved away from the establishment to new things, beginning with coming to a new land and casting off the shackles of foreign rule. As the old system is learned, a new and rival institution is opened. Most of the CHURCHES that exist today are a result of reaction to existing religious bodies. True Christianity is supposed to change people and as people change, they are normally not satisfied with older more structured ways. The same is true within the church. The younger evangelical and community churches, together with Para-church groups, are ministering to the needs and concerns of the people. This should not surprise anyone. The grass-roots effort at renewal is a continuing process; it is part of the Protestant spirit. The old-line CHURCHES would be wise to utilize the process and renew the structures and processes within the church that minister to the people.

A lack of agreement concerning doctrine and the mixed message contributes to the exclusivity of most congregations. With all the public fan fare about equality and unity in Christ, the silent message is one of exclusion. Inclusion as an active concept is lost in the subliminal message of the architecture, the program, and the general atmosphere of the local congregation.

With an emphasis on doctrine and difference, there is little effort to understand the various cultures that make up the church or the community. This, together with a concentration on programs and activities, causes both individuals and families to be neglected. An over powering concern for numbers and buildings makes the congregation a stew pot rather than a blending of cultures under the banner of Christianity. There will always be ethnic and cultural differences in a pluralistic society, but an emphasis on people rather than an institution could create an atmosphere conducive to growth and development of a Christian congregation. There will never be a total melting of all cultures into one unit. Differences must be lessened and common ground emphasized in an effort to find fundamental assumptions that support the common Christian foundation upon which to build a church that ministers to all the people in a particular community on the basis of quality rather than quantity.

IX. CONGREGATIONS FAIL TO AMPLIFY QUALITY

Churches seek quantity rather than quality.

A Christian congregation should be both adequate and effective. Quality and quantity are mutually exclusive; increase one, decrease the other. There must be proportional balance between these two elements to maintain a viable state in any organization. The dynamic aspect of organizational growth and development goes through predictable stages. A failure to understand these phases locks the thinking of a congregation into fixed attitudes that handicap the effectiveness of group function.

All phases of growth are temporary; consequently, there is no continuous growth. This aspect of growth must be understood to avoid obstructions to development and adequacy. The constant effort to push quantity causes organized religion to neglect the quality needed to support and strengthen the basic fabric of Christianity. Striving to build the largest church in town or an effort of one local church to attempt all ministry normally left to an organized group of churches, brings to mind the dreams of the builders of the Titanic.

The Titanic's builders wanted to build the largest ship in the world. This was a noble goal, but their ego was larger than the shipbuilding technology of that day. Why did the Titanic sink? It hit an iceberg--not really. It sank after it hit an iceberg, but because it was constructed too large for the quality of the steel from which it was made. It sank because the lookout in the crow's-nest was alert and signaled the bridge so the ship could turn in an effort to avoid the obstruction. The lookout was correct to warn the bridge. The crew was correct in turning sharply. Had the ship rammed head on into the iceberg it probably would have remained afloat, or at least it would have taken longer to sink and many passengers could have been saved. By sideswiping the iceberg, the hull was damaged, rivets popped, and the quality of steel was unable to withstand the pressure.

The steel in the ship was brittle and could not absorb the massive amounts of pressure brought on by cold water that filled compartments. The ship literally broke apart. The real problem was high sulfur content of the steel from which the ship was constructed. This made the steel fracture in cold water under pressure. The steel makers used the best technology available and thought they had done a good job. They did not understand the concept of brittle fracture caused by high sulfur content in steel. In reality, the shipbuilding design and technology were ahead of the knowledge of the steel makers. Those who made the steel were long dead before the technology was advanced sufficiently to explain the disaster. The steel with which the ship was built was not declared the reason for the disaster until eight decades after the ship went to the bottom of the sea.

The largest ship of the day, designed to be unsinkable, sank within three hours of hitting the iceberg. Some of the richest men in the world went down with the ship's captain and the architect who designed the unsinkable Titanic.   The sinking of the Titanic made changes in shipbuilding, the procedures for handling lifeboats, and in maritime communication. Yet, it was several generations before shipbuilding steel advanced sufficiently to meet the dreams of the architect or the maritime company who built the Titanic.

The moral of the Titanic is that dreams or visions may not be enough. It is not sufficient to have a good idea; one must understand the consequences of the idea. Even doing one's job well is not sufficient to avert human disaster. The steel makers, the ship builders, or even the alertness of the lookout in the crow's nest, or the quick and proper response of the crew on the bridge, could not make a difference in the design or the faulty material with which the architect's dream boat was constructed. It also suggested that the problems of life should be faced head on and the consequences taken.   Usually, attempts to avert disaster fail because of previous errors in judgment or planning.

Those who plan and develop structures of religious organizations could learn from the Titanic disaster.   Size and money did not make a difference. Personalities and the rich and famous with money did not make a difference. Many of the plans from the past organizations built on the reputation and good name of previous leaders are simply accidents waiting to happen. The structures of the past do not adequately inform the present.   Even religious organizations are made of human design and limited by the human element.   Regardless of the spiritual nature of the enterprise, the human factor is always a liability. It is an amazing fact that some Church leaders feel they can minister to and shepherd thousands of members on the journey to spiritual fulfillment. Have they forgotten that Jesus Christ Himself consistently taught only twelve, that the congregations of Bible days were small house churches filled with the zeal and power of a first generation experience?   Jesus actually attempted to cut the size of His crowd down.

He saw the crowd as following for the "loaves and fishes." On one occasion, only three disciples remained and Jesus told them to go away, too. Peter declared, "Where are we going to go, you have the Words of Life"; consequently, the decision of Peter, James, and John to stay near to Christ was honored. This was an effort to improve the quality and exactly the opposite of growth in numbers. When considering the quality of Christian commitment in the context of this leadership example, it is no wonder so many leaders fail to achieve their lofty goals.

Organizational growth is not distinct; it follows the pattern of nature. Constructive coordination of differing facets into a complete and cohesive unit gives rise to healthy development in early rapid growth. Growth is not confined to the early stages, but the rate of growth is affected by the developmental phase in which growth occurs. Some growth may continue as long as there is vitality, but mature growth has more to do with function than with size. A young organization may be evaluated based on size, but mature units are judged on the basis of quality.

An organism and an organization continue to grow through cell enlargement and cell duplication. This is part of the maturing and reproductive process and does not always work adequately. In fact, in Living Systems Theory the reproductive aspect of a "living system" is the only part of the critical process that does not have to work to remain viable. A state of growth exists in both an organism and an organization where the unit is alive and well, but does not reproduce itself.

The original unit itself may not continue to develop in size. Age retards the aspect of growth that contributes to size, but change continues to be present until death of the organism or the deterioration of the organization. Within this continuity, there are many metamorphosis-like critical periods of discontinued growth. One thing is certain: the process of growth is dynamic and the phases or stages normally relate to strengthening of the unit rather than to the size.

All growth follows the S-curve normally seen in plant and animal development. The curve also exists in the life of human groups and organizations. The shape of the normal growth curve reveals a similarity between the growth curve of units and the whole. The growth of religious institutions and local congregations follows a similar curve. This growth curve has two opposing forces: a self-accelerating slope and a self-inhibiting slope.

A constant rate of growth is normally observed until the "frontier land" or the available resources, both human and material, are exhausted. Then, following the use of all easily accessible resources, the growth-retarding factors initiate the declining slope. At this juncture the organization must mobilize all available resources to move forward or an institutionalization stagnation effect will overcome the forward progress and an inevitable decline begins.

Success normally contains the seeds of failure; consequently, growth itself creates a condition that may retard the process in accordance with the law of diminishing returns. The perpetual renewal of the whole structure is imperative to continue to support growth and development, but the tendency is for this renewal to be at an ever-decreasing rate. This is caused by the deterioration and hardening of the vital structures of growth by leadership that does not clearly understand the process. Slowing of the process, with consequent increasing frequency of decay in various functions and facilities of either an organism or an organization, reflects this loss of elasticity. Normally, it takes drastic action and concerted effort to push through the natural block and continue the expected growth.

Continued growth is not inherent in nature or in the structure of social institutions. In the wild, one does not normally discover a lion or zebra that has continued to grow much beyond the normal size of the group. Even among domesticated animals, cows in a herd are about the same size and chickens in the barnyard are relatively the same in size and weight. Trees in a forest normally have a fixed size for the area or region. Corn growing in a field is about the same size, and the seed, soil, and weather determine this size. A farmer can do little when defective seed, poor soil, or bad weather limits the crop. A similar process exists in social organizations of human society.

Nature nourishes trees with a supply of watery liquid called sap. It moves upward in part through an intricate supply system with decreasing pressure. The taller a tree becomes the more difficult the natural supply of nourishing becomes. Even a vacuum pump is limited to pulling water higher than about 36 feet.

Sap-lifting forces created by evaporation and transpiration sustain trees that are taller than those adequately supplied with sap. This is a kind of breathing water through the leaves. In addition, adhesion and cohesion due to the stickiness of molecules in the fluid-carrying vessels nourish growth. It is complicated. The basic rise of the watery fluid is rapid; however, the other nourishing processes are much slower. In reality, the larger the tree grows the more difficult the nourishing process. This is especially true of fruit-bearing trees. Since the church is called a "garden" and the kingdom is compared to a Mustard tree in scripture, the same is probably true of a church as a fruit-bearing entity.

A tree grows in the roots (a supply system), just beneath the bark (a support system), and at the terminal bud at the end of the limbs (a foliage and fruit-bearing system). The constant pruning of fruit trees keeps them within the natural size to receive nourishment from the root system. The church must be aware of complications of size. Could this be a reason for smaller churches bearing more fruit than the larger ones? Research has demonstrated the viability of individual witness through a small church to produce converts when compared with a staff oriented program of larger congregations. Size does affect fruit-bearing.

There may be foliage, the appearance of life and the promise of fruit, but fruit is limited. From the ministry of Jesus, the church must learn that leaves alone are not sufficient; there must be fruit. Jesus cursed the fig tree that had leaves but no fruit. What are the implications of this for the church?

In plant and animal life, there are limits to size. It has been estimated that wood fiber could support the growth of a tree up to about 300 feet. The giant redwood trees of California stand high above all other trees on the planet, but they have not reached the limitation of 300 feet. The dinosaurs were of enormous size but they are now extinct. Speculation is that the climate changed and food became limited; consequently, dinosaurs are gone and are relics of a bygone age. They are reconstructed now for museum presentation from fragments of bone. Scientists can determine from the size and structure of skeletal remains the normal size of the animal. Limits of structure and environment are obvious and applicable to human organizations as well as to both present and extinct plants and animals.

In examining the organizations of society, a distinct pattern emerges. Initial growth occurs as the carrying capacity of the social habitat is approached; the rate of growth decreases and normally leads to an organization of a fixed size. If the social habitat is destroyed, changed or drastically altered, the organization decreases in proportion to the decrease in carrying capacity. At times this seems to be an inevitable process; however, those organizations with a spiritual purpose may have the unusual assistance of divine power to cope with the problem of diminished growth.

Notwithstanding the limitations of a fixed environment, provided an organization can adjust to the changing habitat, it may survive, even stabilize and become fixed in size but may be considerably smaller than its true potential had the resources and habitat been unlimited. An example is the Swedish Baptist Church that began to die in America because the number of available Swedes declined.   A name change and a mission to reach a larger population were effective in extending the life and effectiveness of the small denomination.

A look at the three main phases of a normal growth pattern makes the process of organizational growth easier to understand. There is a period of preparation for growth sometimes called the "lag phase." The time of actual growth is called the exponential or logarithmic phase and climaxes in maximum efficiency.   This phase usually gives way to healthy development. A constructive coordination of differing facets of the organization creates a uniform whole. When normal development has reached the extent of resources or environment, a stationary or institutional phase usually develops because of the efforts of the organization to survive.

The transition to the institutional phase is a turning point for the organization and can become a terminal phase for the institution. During this critical phase of development, the organization loses its flexibility and operations settle down to routine and often reactionary activities. This crisis is met by channeling the energies and resources previously used for growth and expansion into the creation of institutional structures designed to maintain the status quo.   Leaders begin to concentrate on programs and projects that reflect their personalities and "simulate" progress. Sometimes it actually worked, but at other times the bitter seeds of limited expectations works to defeat the most noble of efforts. At this point, for religious and educational institutions, it is time to seek divine intervention.

This final phase is a leveling off period when growth ceases and the size stabilizes. In secular organizations this usually calls for mergers, name changes, diversification, or some campaign to influence the public that their product or service is new and improved and therefore better or best, or a least different and consequently better. The application to religious organizations or Christian congregations is apparent.

Developmental growth creates both formal and informal structures. The formal features of the organization are characterized by a command and task structure while friendship and interest dominate the informal aspects of the process. This structure is modified progressively by processes operating within the organization as it evolves into an institution. If the organization survives entrance into the institutional stage, formal rules are increasingly imposed upon members that are no longer a product of primarily voluntary interaction. Rigid administration of both procedure and process tends to increase efficiency for a time, but ultimately, it produces a vicious cycle that impairs the effectiveness of the organization. Unless there is a relaxation of the formal aspects and an increase of the informal facets, the organization may collapse. In a best case scenario, the organization may find a size and continue for a time to be relatively effective with a limited constituency.

Cooperation and interdependency are necessary in all areas of religious institutions. Growth in numbers, without consideration of the effect on quality, limits real progress in development. In spite of obstacles to quality, Christian organizations seem determined to increase size and budget without an adequate agenda for using either. This breeds unnecessary competition and personal strife among membership and frustrates the whole function of the organization for the benefit of the people.

Perhaps a reminder that to serve an organization in administration is "to serve" the needs of the constituency. It does not mean, "to grow" unless the needs of present members can be met within the context of growth. Since there seems to be no adequate way to measure quality of a religious organization, the process is surrogated to an assessment of size or phony-religiosity. This means counting noses and nickels and depending on budgets and buffets. Each organization can create its on criteria for being religious and project the belief that compliance with the formal aspects of this criteria makes one a better organization than others who follow another pattern.

The anticipatory aspects of growth are often neglected. Growth causes an institution or organization to become more costly to operate and in the end less effective in many ways. One distinguishing feature characterizing normal developmental growth is the anticipation of future needs, not only for the individual but also for the institution. When planning becomes limited enough to cut off from view the long-ranged negative consequences of the growth, genuine progress has been drastically impeded.

In considering a church as a "social institution," David O. Moberg determined five stages in the growth and development of an organization. The stages were (1) weak association, (2) formal organization, (3) maximum efficiency (4) institutional stage, and (5) disintegration. These steps seem to suggest an ultimate demoralization of an organization and the ultimate disintegration of an institution. This is not inevitable; purposeful action can alter the future of an institution.

Several decades ago, Findley B. Edge in a quest for vitality in religion wondered if the tide of institutionalism could be stemmed and the experiential, individual religious experience be preserved within the context of American Christianity.   This question remains a perplexing dilemma for which Christianity has found no solution. Growth will create changes together with some negative consequences. When a group accepts a smaller number than the leader desires, it affects the positional ego and complicates the ministry of presence required to produce effective leadership in a religious organization.   The alternatives are equally undesirable.

Some years ago, my speaking at a Canadian Church Growth Conference created a discussion about the size of a church. In reviewing my philosophy of growth, someone suggested that my view depreciated the large super-church in favor of the small community congregation. The question was asked "How large should a church be?" My response was, "How large should a cow be?" The questioner responded that he did not know. The group was asked if they were required to determine the normal size of a cow, how one could go about the process. It was suggested that perhaps one should observe and count some cows to determine the average or normal size. The apparent answer was that most mature cows were about the same size.

My next question was "What if you owned a cattle ranch and discovered a cow in the pasture that was 25 times larger than all the other cows, what would you do?" A participant answered, "I would get it out of the pasture as quickly as possible before it stepped on the other cows." Exactly, this is the same about the super-church. If not in the process of becoming an abnormally large church, then soon after, other smaller congregations in the area would be trampled. This fact exists. Research demonstrated that in one southern city a large Baptist church had brought about the demise of thirteen other small Baptist churches. It is the law of the sea: big fish eat little fish. The application to congregation size was evident.

This is not to claim that a religious order or organization must lose the life and dynamics that nurtured it through periods of privation and persecution. When the changes that naturally occur in organizations are not understood, leaders are blind to the reality that organizations often deteriorate and fail in the fulfillment of their initial mission. History indicates religious movements such as Judaism, Early Christianity, the Church of the Reformation, and many modern CHURCHES began as vital, dynamic movements, but over time lapsed into cold, lifeless formalism as they matured into institutions. This does not mean that there was no life left in such an organization, it simply means that growth was limited to the resources and the environment in which an organization existed.

All growth is not good. The young are measured in terms of size and weight, but a mature adult would normally not be characterized in society by size. Of course, there are exceptions. Some athletes are identified by size and weight, but there are known health and social problems related to success in certain sports. The linebacker on the football team or a heavyweight boxer may have a few moments of glory, but these are short lived. Fame and health are here today and gone tomorrow. Aside from the monetary rewards, most healthy Americans would not wish to walk in their shoes or take the risks and punishment which characterizes these achievements.

Unbridled or uncontrolled growth in humans is both malignant and destructive. Unlimited growth is characterized as abnormal and is considered a source of evil or anguish. Has the unlimited growth of the American government been good? Has the unlimited growth of one aspect of the economy not been harmful? Anti-trust laws protect trade and commerce from unlawful monopolies and unbridled growth of one aspect of business. Christian congregations need to understand the risks of growth in quantity without improvement in the quality of the operation or service.

Why should a religious order or organization be judged by numerical size, the square feet of a facility, or the nature of the architecture? What about outcomes in relation to mission? What about the quality of ministry and service to a constituency? What about fruit bearing and harvest? What about a worthy contribution to society? What about genuine service to mankind? What about the non-quantitative "spiritual" aspects of the group? To determine value or worth by numbers, whether people or dollars, is to devalue the worth of religion in society and to demean the sacrificial service of dedicated individuals who have unselfishly served others without asking for earthly reward.

Worship is a response to the "worth-ship of God" not to the size of the congregation or the nature of the budget. How much is God worth in the life of an individual or a congregation? This may not be measurable by scientific means, and may not be evident to the public, but it certainly exists. A Christian congregation should be evaluated on the bases of the quality of ministry and service to the community, not on attendance, baptisms or budgets. Without an emphasis on the qualitative aspects of organizational development, growth in numbers alone can become a liability to a local congregation.

The future impact of Christian institutions on American life will depend more on the quality of ministry to people and the nature of services provided to the community than meeting attendance or the size of the budget. All organizations should be measured by the quality of their product and on a substantial contribution to the welfare of their constituency in a given community. When this occurs the Christian message has substance.

X. CONGREGATIONS FAIL TO ASSURE SUBSTANCE

Churches advance structure rather than substance.

The message of organized religion is always confused by the past. The facts of each story point to a living with, living down or living up to the past. This so complicates the present message as to make it void of current value to many people. The differences on the one hand and the similarity on the other repudiate expressions as to the viability of the local church. Religion clearly has a future, but a conclusive statement regarding the future of the local church in a pluralistic society may not be predicted from the existing data.

There is too much controversial evidence, too many different opinions to make a conclusive statement about the future of Christianity in America. Only God can see the future. The work of God will not fail. Individual churches, local congregations may fail to adequately reach their communities for Christ, but the message of Grace will be propagated. It will not come by the might of a great preacher or the program of the institutional church, but by the Spirit of God working though believing individuals who are committed to share their faith in the world.

Local congregations are preoccupied with building design, polity, organizational patterns, governing structures, arrangement of furniture and the order of service to be concerned with the essence of Christian faith. The complex compositions of past knowledge, used as the basic elements of religion, are not adequate representations of the essential elements or substance of Christianity. Even a combination of these elements with known traditions does not adequately inform one of the fundamental essences of Christianity.

The evidence is clear: Christianity is artificially divided into two camps. The artificial dichotomy of the universal church has been divided into catholic and protestant. While Catholic congregations maintain a semblance of public unity, Protestant churches are obviously further divided until the central idea of their existence is confused by a muddled message. The population has either misunderstood or discarded both the meaning and the process. This is not unique to Christianity. All the great religions show a gap between the teachings and writings of chief exponents and the congregants. It is logical to assume that congregations at a particular place of worship often fail to live the message proclaimed by the spiritual leader. The existence of this gap is often ignored.

Leaders influenced by the past control congregations. Ancient and historical religions have also contributed to the function of many churches. Since the local church was the social and administrative unit of much of Europe in the past, immigrants and literature from the past have affected the American church. Christianity in Europe, and other religions in distant parts of the world, influenced the rhythm of life by religious festivals, seasonal events, and teachings that affected the family and the life of individuals. Existing data does not fully assess how the Middle Ages infected Christianity with its pagan beliefs and practices, including sorcery, witchcraft and fertility rites, but these are evident.

A denomination or sect is a system of religious thought. The existence of a denomination, or even the most eccentric of sects, is usually formed because of criticism or conflict with institutional religion. Consequently, as the most personal of Faiths matures, it becomes more institutionalized and has within it the seeds of its own deterioration. What is common to all religions and particularly a local place of worship is concern for people and their needs? Beliefs held and institutions created by human beings in turn receive a part of the substance that creates distinctive cultures.

Scholars of religion see the institutional church as part of the difficulty. Unless the church is viewed as part of organized religion, it can never be understood. The professional leadership that has emerged in relation to all organized religion is never popular for long anywhere. Fear and suspicion of power is worldwide and well founded. The noblest of intentions or teachings have not prevented the abuse of power by some that suppose to mediate divine mysteries to the population.

The accumulation of wealth by institutions, rather than using resources for the stated spiritual mission is disconcerting to the population. The deadening weight of custom and the inflexibility of religious bureaucracy have contributed to the loss of influence by the local church. Consequently, there have been upheavals in the name of reform that divided most CHURCHES. Even in clergy controlled CHURCHES, the clergy themselves have imposed limitations on the number of years or terms an elected official may serve in an ecclesiastical leadership position. Tight hierarchical structures are open to certain abuses and democratic ones to others. The move to limit time in office is part of a protest movement against organized religious power even by those who aspire to attain and use such power themselves.

When the protest movement does not work adequately or fast enough to satisfy those who aspire to power, frequently the organization is split and new religious organizations formed. This provides positions of power for the king makers. The cycle is vicious and destructive to the influence of Christianity because of the negative effect on the individuals who invest life and service in organized religion. In such a way, they start as the inheritor of a long tradition of wariness toward the cause they wish to lead. They may sincerely want to influence and serve the constituency, but often simply add to the process of alienation of the people from the basic mission of the church. Expectation and disappointment in part compounds the suspicion. The recurring idea that "things ought to be otherwise" and the willingness of individuals to struggle to make things different has, in a few instances, brought new life to institutions. Nevertheless, the change is short lived and the cycle normally repeats itself.

Opinion is no substitute for serious research, but the sociologists who study the church confront historical dimensions of organized religion and never see the whole picture. The past is such a part of the present that the future is unclear from the data. What sorts of people belong to a particular church? How is authority distributed and used? Where does the money come from and where does it go? What are the relationships between the congregation and the local community? An adequate evaluation requires these and a host of other facts. The sad truth is that most answers to the above questions have such a spin that the "spin doctors" of politics could envy the skill.

The most complex idea of religion is how to make the teachings of a particular church the personal property of the individual. The effort to make religion a matter of personal commitment in faith and action is most difficult as social conformity declines in society. Although church attendance may be important, it is not all consuming or transforming enough to precipitate adequate change in the daily life of the individual. The teachings of the church do not become the substance of the participant's life. Most individuals are unable to accept wholly the doctrines taught by their church or denomination.

Notwithstanding this limitation, many individuals find religious questions of overpowering importance to them intellectually and spiritually. On this basis, such folk may take a moral stand justified on fundamentally religious ground. The attempt may be to reinterpret an old faith so it does not ask them to either abandon the modern world or to accept it on its own terms. The effort is to reinterpret religious ideas in non-theistic and evolutionary terms to satisfy humanist concerns in society.

A trend exists in America that in the matter of religion one person's opinion is as good as any other. Such individualism is a phenomenon of modern society with its mobility and rootless nature. In particular, the mobility of American society has affected religion. As individuals and families move from place to place, they attend different churches. As they intermarry, one may be a Baptist, the other a Methodist, so they compromise and attend a Lutheran or Presbyterian Church with almost no regard for theology or doctrine. This trend began as America moved from rural areas or small towns to the city. This much is sociologically verifiable by census and other data: whatever the religious affiliation may have been, most people tend to abandon it when they move from one place to another. No wonder the children are confused and uncomfortable in the church.

A national poll confirmed the dilemma that showed more people "prayed" than believed there was a "God." To whom did they pray? When a majority believe in God and continue to demand separation of Church and State, but want the state to institute "prayer in public schools," do they understand the responsibility for praying with children is a parental role? When there is little difference in the moral and ethical standards of those within and without the organized church, one must ask: "What is the value?" Have religious leaders exaggerated the differences of belief inside and outside the church?

With wavering allegiance of parents to the church, how can one expect children to choose the path of the organized church? In fact, church attendance includes the very young and the very old with few between. The most active of home builders and caregivers to children are not present. The most influential people in the community, those who run the government and lead the corporations, are conspicuously absent in the week to week participation. If they participate at all, it is on special occasions when it is a personal asset or benefit to their position in the community. The true nature of personal commitment is not evident.

Some pessimists would say the church has no future in America, but this denies the force of faith and the strength of history to impact society. Others observe the decline of religious observance and the weakness of religious institutions in society and say that which will exist in the future will be a weakened version of the weakness that presently exists. The secular optimists see that government and other agencies perform many functions the church used to do. Some claim an observable decay in the need to believe. Others point to certain factors in society that once required a religious explanation and no longer demand one. The conclusion is that if people do not need to believe, this justifies predicting a time when people will not believe. Believing, however, is difficult to assess.

Freud wrote that as men realized that the desire for a God was the longing of weak and defenseless human beings for an almighty father and that as they admitted that their religion was childish thinking, it would die away. Freud was wrong, yet his theories about thinking are still current. His reputation as a skilled analyst and as a writer may somewhat account for his ideas remaining current, but he may have been partly right: the wish that religion were dead is widespread.

Marx wrote, "Religion was the sigh of the oppressed creature, the heart of a heartless world, the spirit of soulless stagnation, the opium of the people." Lenin reinterpreted Marx's words with a venomous hatred of religion. Marx felt that religion would disappear in a classless society because there would be no need for it. Traces of his influence still exist in general theory outside the countries once dominated by communism, probably because of past clergy exploitation and the generalizing from historical evidence that the church in history once kept the people in intellectual darkness thus hindering human progress and enlightenment.

One would assume from the known facts that Faith was dead in the old Soviet Union. Yet on the very day the USSR legally died, the former Foreign Minister returned to the church for baptism and support. Does this point to a dormant faith, although not outwardly practiced, was yet alive and searching for expression? The academic community has been an arena where it was not popular to express ones personal faith or to question when science infringed on personal faith and reality. In a 1949 high school science text, the explanation for atomic energy included the phrase "and other God like chemicals and actions." A present public school text would not include such a statement.

The law and custom prohibits the expression of personal faith. Yet, the fact that it does not appear in print does not deny the existence of faith in the heart of the author. Consequently, one cannot judge the strength of personal commitment by current societal standards. One can only make assumptions based on an evaluation of the organized church and the strength of its performance in the community and society.

Religion is recognized as important to the early stages of human development: language, conceptual thinking and social organization. This widespread conception of religion, as essentially part of man's early history which is logically left behind in the process of human evolution, is a major problem. The purposive control advocates of human development give man responsibility for the course of personal development. The determinists claim man has no choice but to follow the path that leads to less and less religious expression in personal and community life. Yet, there is toughness in religion regardless of its form of expression. It persists and will continue to be a part of the human equation. The obvious conclusion is that what continues will be less organized and more personalized. Is this far from early expressions of faith in the New Testament? Could the progressive decline of the organized church be part of a cycle that could take mankind back to personal faith and the moral practice of innate ethics?

The old generalization that more civilizations perished from internal decay than from external enemies seems to bid bad news for local congregations. The weakness of individual commitment poses the major difficulty for the church. Through Christ, true believers can do anything. This is the hope for the church.

The church may overcome secular society, political encroachment, confusing doctrine, and weak leaders, but it can never fully overcome the weakness of personal Christian experience and witness. Individual believers will determine the purpose and progress of the church, not her enemies.

The present church may not survive, but a Church made of redeemed souls will not only survive; the Church will triumph!   Provided current believers see Christianity as more than a social club, there is hope.   Provided Christianity becomes a lifestyle and not just a self-help process; there is hope.   Provided present believers see Christianity not as just a part of man's history, but as an essential path to God, there is hope. Provided Christianity becomes the means to move towards the achievement of ones full human potential, there is hope.   Provided the church is able to restore basic principles, there is hope. Provided individuals embrace the moral soundness of morality and ethics, there is hope. Provided the church overcomes the adulteration and weakening of basic faith, there is hope. Provided the church rejects pragmatism and embraces principle, there is hope!

XI. CONGREGATIONS FAIL TO ADOPT PRINCIPLES

Churches embrace pragmatism rather than principle.

Leadership in Christianity should personally embrace the principles that undergird the Christian faith. It is a matter of choice, but often the choice is not made to follow the principles by either the leadership or the members of local congregations. Many local churches fail to accept the authenticity of scripture and the essence of faith is not used as a basis for reason or conduct. Religious leaders should remember that a failed construct of Communism was "The end justifies the means." Just because a process or procedure works for the moment does not mean that it is good for the church over time.

The functional criterion should be principle before pragmatism. The measure of scriptural teachings should be the driving force in Christianity, not the latest marketing surveys or consumer trends. Pragmatism has triumphed over principle repeatedly as religious leaders look to public opinion to guide decisions. Form and function work together to facilitate social change, but methodology alone cannot transform a gathering of strangers into a community of saints.   God uses people, but people use methods. In the early church, the test of "what works" was the response to the gospel and the acceptance of the claims of Christ on one's life. The programmatic approach to church ministry is a sacrilege. Certainly, the church as a social institution operated by people should cause the human factor to be a part of the planning, but there is a larger issue.   People follow the practices they see validated by the church. When what works influences decisions to increase attendance rather than scriptural standards, the true cause of Christianity is in jeopardy. Consequently, one should not judge a congregation by the size of attendance, but by the character of the people. The quality of participation is important and the standards supporting the behavior of members of the congregation. If the church is to stem the tide of secularization, the functional imperatives must be based on principles.

The percentage of American adults attending religious meetings has been about the same for the past decade. Although about 45% attend religious gathering, the actual membership of Protestant churches has declined in real numbers during the past several decades. A surrogate assessment of religiosity shows alarming concern for the actual level of commitment and a lack of consistent participation. The distribution of this attendance is also a matter of concern. Over half of professing Christians attend less than 10 percent of the churches. This means that 90 percent of the churches are small and struggling.

Most congregations are less that 200 worshipers and this number represents from twenty to 40 percent of the acknowledged membership. Entire congregations plus paid staff involvement win less that five people in a year. The whole of an organized congregation is doing less than one new convert of past generations. With the limited birth rate in America, this style of corporate ministry does not even replace the deaths.   Converts to Christianity have always been the result of individual believers doing the work of evangelism. Tragically, individuals no longer witness effectively by their lifestyle. The church accepted this delegated task, but has failed to carry it out effectively. In the past, individuals did better than the organized church is doing today.   What does this say for the future?

In the past two decades, about 4,000 super congregations have emerged on the American scene.   This growth from about 100 such churches with more than 2,000 members to the present number speaks volumes for the trend in American congregations. Super-churches are not evangelizing; they are simply adding the disgruntled members who have deserted smaller churches. It is a "musical pew" version of the game "musical chairs" children played at parties in previous generations. True one-on-one evangelism and consistent disciple-making are not happening in America. Methodology and growth strategy have replaced spiritual excitement and commitment to reaching friends and family with the gospel. These super-churches are sometimes doing things that smaller congregations could not do, but at what cost to the true nature of the community church and its mission of individual participation.

As the number of large congregations increase, the smaller churches decrease. For each super-church that emerges, about 100 smaller churches seriously decline and/or die. Since little true evangelism is taking place, the number of believers is not increasing; consequently, the appearance of American Christianity is changing. No longer does the community church exist that was a gathering of family and friends genuinely concerned about the needs of one another. The church has become a place where strangers meet in a holy club setting. Those who gather are lost in the sea of faces and have become spectators without spiritual commitment. Without active participators in lifestyle evangelism, the church has little future. With declining attendance and half-empty churches, the image of an effective church is lost. As American churches decline, they hinder the world effort of missions and evangelism.

Denominational models, with a franchised program, are not the way to base the operation of religious congregations on principles. Operating from a principled base rather than models is the answer. The early believers of the New Testament did not have models, just basic principles enhanced by personal experience and genuine commitment. The context of each local congregation was different.

When Dietrich Bonhoeffer faced death in a Nazi prison in the closing days of World War II, it was because of his personal resistance to Hitler's decrees related to the German church. Through the Confessing Church, which resisted governmental infringement, Bonhoeffer began to develop constructs for principled responsibility in relation to the Christian life. During his imprisonment, Bonhoeffer further developed a personalized approach to Christianity. He expressed a different perspective of life and religion in his prison letters to Eberhard Bethge, a trusted friend. Although Bonhoeffer made fragmentary hints about a time when there would be no religion at all, these statements concerned the reality of Christian faith, not the formal, public expression of religion. He believed that religion had an antecedent obligation that binds men as a social force to certain responsibility. He suggested that the meanness of war annihilated this viable historical possibility of religion. Looking at the tragedy of war, Bonhoeffer understood that Christian preaching and theology did not create a human conscience to prevent the inhumanity of armed conflict during the decades of two world wars. The armed conflict crushed the internal principles by which Christians engaged and interfaced peoples of the world.

Bonhoeffer, in an early mention of the new "religion-less world" (30 April 1944) suggested that men in the future would speak of God in a secular manner rather than as theologians. He not only raised the possibility of different means of expressing religious language, but that it would be without the old presuppositions and institutional aspects of the organized church. Bonhoeffer pointed to the time when Christianity would return to the individual level of faith and practice based on biblical principles rather than the institutionalized format that persists in Western culture.

Bonhoeffer's letters pointed to a confidence that "religion" was to be and should be an expression of personal godliness rather than the teachings of an organized church. His writings suggested that nurturing the institutional church would not complete an individual's life. This fulfillment comes only by the addition of God to life through an individual experience. This conflicted with the pragmatism of modern religious philosophy that attempts to manage and manipulate the behavior of man. Such efforts fail to understand the historical reality of the human race. The effort to manipulate does not produce a different person, because the teachings degenerate into a kind of secular religion. This produces a fatherless fantasy and adulterated religiosity.

Man is not free of religion today. Modern ideologies have expressed and extended their hold on the population through the institutionalization of religion. Bonhoeffer claimed that the world had learned to cope with important questions without recourse to God as a working hypothesis (8 June 1944). This idea troubled Bonhoeffer during the final days before his execution at the hands of the Gestapo. He struggled with poetry and letters in a rush to leave a legacy for the German church.

One day following devotions using Numbers 11:23 and II Corinthians 1:20, Bonhoeffer wrote about the promise God gave Moses about Divine deliverance. In this devotional mode, he wrote (21 August 1944) about the believer's "final amen" in Christ and made an appeal for personal Christianity. He postulated that believers must repeatedly immerse themselves in the "life, sayings, deeds, suffering and death of Jesus, to know what God promises and fulfills... again in these turbulent times we lose sight of why it is really worth living." Had Bonhoeffer survived the war, many believed he would have continued this effort to redirect the German church toward a more personalized lifestyle of piety and witness.

The same is true today. There are no universal models. The constant experimentation with the structural practicalities of the local congregation to bring it in line with the norms of current society has muddled the sense of mission for the church. The abandoned house churches of the New Testament became a secular cathedral. Without a spiritual anchor in a raging sea of social change, the identity and function of individuals are confused. Action, based on scriptural principles and genuine concern for people, is the only answer to the decline seen in current congregations and is the only real hope for constructive social change.

The true growth of the past took place in small congregations. The super-churches of today are "gathering" the harvest of seeds planted by the ministers and members of struggling churches. What will happen when the super-church gobbles up the small churches? Will anyone remain to plant the "seed corn"? Perhaps the large congregation that upwardly delegates the entire ministry to a paid staff will eat the seed corn or leave it stored in the church crib.

What about a future harvest for the super-church to gather? There will be no harvest without the primary work of individuals. The passing of time has reinforced the troublesome observation that super-congregations and popular preachers simply draw from other churches and in fact weaken the total impact of Christianity. The effort of the super-congregation has not increased the total number of active participants in worship.

Being lost in the crowd becomes an attraction to many members of a community church. This precipitates a lessening of responsibility and personal commitment to Christianity. As people move to different churches, those left behind have become discouraged thinking those who moved on have become less faithful. This diminishes the crucial fervor of the local church for evangelism and missions. The overall estrangement with the church by the American population has not changed. The principles of Christianity are not adequately working within the Protestant movement. Somehow, the movement must get back to the roots that caused the Reformers to embrace certain sure and firm principles.

The Reformers were personally embracing the essence of Christianity and applying the fundamental nature to their lives. It worked for a while; now believers must return to the basics of personal Christianity instead of being lost in a corporate structure and institutional manipulation. The practices handed down from the Reformers are a heritage worth preserving. Past generations do have a message for the present church, but that message is not to preserve every word they wrote, but to follow the principles by which they dealt with the needs of their generation.

A process or procedures, for today, based on the Christian heritage of the Reformers, may not be sufficient; the action must be based on principles and deal with the present problems in a meaningful way. The attitude, a predisposition to act responsibly and timely, to resist the evil of structures that impinge on religious freedom should be part of the heritage that drives the present need for change. Sectarian restraints conflict with the present need to advance beyond the usual limits of religious reformation. The present generation calls out for spiritual renewal.   True spiritual heritage of past generations should guide this renewal.   Leaders ought to take hold of current issues and deal from personal convictions to cause needed change. Surely, the corporate structure of organized religion cannot produce meaningful change to meet the spiritual needs of the present generation.   There must be a better way.   The answer is basic, personalized Christianity with historical roots and a rich heritage.

Individuals, following the example of Bonhoeffer and others, must attack the evils of the present society that threaten the integrity of the church. The challenge of Bonhoeffer's life and practical theology deals with discipleship and ethics and speaks directly to the needs of the Christian community today. A willingness to take risks that come from a devotional and principled heart is necessary to capture the spirit of Bonhoeffer. His writings provide a new perspective about Christian worship and personal Christian behavior.

Coming together to worship is both biblical and needed to encourage, edify, and equip the Family of God to function adequately within contemporary society. This does not alter the need for the development of a Christian lifestyle by individual believers.   The church must reach deeply into Christian heritage and develop a corporate worship and individual behavior based on biblical principles.

The practice of pragmatism must not determine the criteria for spiritual knowledge or the operational definitions for biblical principles and values. The church must develop a functional implementation of the common Christian heritage acquired from past generations.

Such functionality requires scriptural principles and expressions compatible with the culture of the local church community. It requires a mixture of race, culture and ethnicity that is homogeneous to the community and harmonious with the gospel for the present generation. Church leadership must guard against arbitrary changes that encroach on the basic heritage of the people.

XII. CONGREGATIONS FAIL TO ACCENT HERITAGE

Churches sanction politics rather than heritage.

Christianity has been an effective instrument in social change in some aspects of society, but the church has all but ignored many aspects of heritage and imposed programs that have been counter productive. Practices that are handed down from the past by tradition become customary behavior that is normally respected by the next generation. The church must respect these traditions and work within the framework of one's heritage in presenting the gospel. The church is a source of positional authority in the community and individuals become emotional and political in their social relations with the power of the church.

Many of the characteristics of a particular population are inherited and reinforced by family and community. To impose a program or procedure on a community that is contrary to custom weakens the influence of the church. When the local heritage is ignored and traditional orientations are replaced, the church will fail to adequately cultivate the population for Christ.

Changing words or programs does not necessarily change people. Traditions are important and should be considered in the process of change. The past should set the tone for all efforts at social change. An attitude is a predisposition to act and relates directly to predictable behavior. Many personal beliefs are not founded on proof or certainty, but are just part of the fabric of one's life. Opinions one holds with respect to questions of family, culture, and religion cannot be changed easily.   Just changing programs or passing laws has never removed the prejudice of the past. Revising history would not change the past. It is people who must be changed; then circumstances will change as people change. This is healthy change. It was not made by decree, but by facilitating changes within individuals and groups.

An old adage that came into modern use in an abbreviated form: prayer changes things, illustrates the point. Prayer "changes things" is not the whole story.   There is an omission of a logical sequence of words.   Actually the proverb was "Prayer changes people and people change things." Changing a few words here and there can drastically change both the meaning and the understanding. It is also true that individuals change more rapidly than do groups. Therefore, the efforts of a few to change others by altering the words of a confession, doctrinal statement or the lyrics of a song is pushing the dynamics of social change to the limits.

The church must create an atmosphere conducive to social change by demonstrating an understanding of local culture and heritage. The Gospel has often penetrated various cultures without making drastic change in the community. This can be understood when one observes the different cities and cultures, described in the New Testament, in which local churches operated. Each functioned within the atmosphere of the local community and was able to produce change in individuals, if not the community.   Since individuals change more easily and more rapidly than do groups, the focus of the church must be on changing individuals and then these changed persons can effect gradual and acceptable change in the community.   One would hope that the church has learned this lesson through centuries of direct experience, but it has not. The current confusion about changes in church music illustrates this tragic failure.

Christianity has been gender-inclusive. Although scripture claimed that "in Christ there is neither male nor female," the realities of life required the recognition of fatherhood and motherhood. The operational terms father, mother, sister, brother, aunt, uncle, grandfather and grandmother, cannot be eliminated from the language of church without some correspondent weakening of the family structure. To bow to present political correctness could further weaken the strong family role and operational definitions the family has contributed to Christianity from early times. Notwithstanding, this comes at a time when government, together with negative aspects of modern culture, have seriously weakened the family unit.

Balance is required when changing lyrics for social correctness. Consideration for the historical period of the poetry, as well as the value and sense of the words by the group involved, is required.   Archaic language can be distracting, but some changes can be equally distracting. In such cases, the reason for the change must be examined. Political correctness is not a sufficient explanation. Should one adopt the reasoning that some hymns should be abandoned rather than changed? The logic follows that the next effort will be to omit scripture passages with which one disagrees. A simple fact is clear: one cannot extract and disentangle facts from the past. They are ever present and cannot be abandoned any more than the dates of history can be erased.

This trend of gender neutral lyrics reflects a trend of religious groups offering their congregations modernized "politically correct" hymnals. Language that might offend minorities and people with disabilities, such as, "darkness" and "blind" to symbolize spiritual ignorance has often been changed. The word "poor" has also been edited out of some hymnals. Military language is sometimes omitted from the lyrics while poetry by Africans and American Indians is added. Some say it is good and needed, others think it is crazy.

Although congregations are not required to use the revised hymnals, there seems to be an obvious agenda. The effort to balance masculine and feminine images of God and sometimes referring to God as "her" could be construed as advancing the agenda of specific groups or points of view. If this further divides the church or if it further confuses the gender specific roles in the family, what has been gained for Christianity? Christian congregations have enough difficulties these days without those with private social agendas further weakening the church's ability to influence society as to the proper role of the family. In most areas, the congregational response to new hymnals has been mostly negative, yet leadership persists in using these revised editions to advance private agendas.

Christians are normally sensitive to other people and their feelings. Specific tenets and beliefs do not only characterize Christianity; it includes the affective domain as well. The feelings of individuals and groups are important. Christianity has always attracted the poor, the weak, the troubled and those in need of significant change in their life. How does this trend impact this issue? Does it open the door of the church to more dilution and pollution or does it close the door on some of the faithful supporters of the cause? What is the bottom line in all of this?

The results will probably be a net loss for the church and another negative impact on Christianity as a whole. Will those groups so carefully protected by the changes in the hymnals now flock to Christian churches? Will the faithful continue to sing in the choir? Such private and hidden agenda processes of the past have already driven from the church the young, the divorced, the busy professional and a host of others. Will the older generation now be alienated from the church?

The most important fact about Jesus may not be that of male gender, but understanding that he had a mother, brothers, sisters and was known as the "Carpenter's son" is certainly an asset. Many young and lonely have identified with Jesus and claimed the security of an "elder brother." Does placing fewer male images in the church hymnal assist the church with reaching unbelieving fathers, deadbeat dads, or young street gangs with the gospel? Deleting male references to Jesus is not honest historically. He was not only a personality in the Bible; Jesus Christ is a man of history. Could one change the male references to George Washington as the Father of our country and not be ridiculed by the academics? Why then do these modern reformers see the necessity to delete the gender references to Jesus? What is their hidden agenda?

The compromise may be the effort to balance gender language when referring to people.   Instead of "Good Christian men, rejoice." an acceptable change could be "Good Christian, friends, rejoice." This seems to be more in keeping with the gender-inclusive nature of Christianity. When members of the Godhead are gender neutral, the theological and political agendas of a few are encroaching on the traditions that have stabilized the church through the hard times of history. The Bible itself refers to the mothering nature of God and there is nothing drastic about changing "Merciful Father" to "Merciful God." The logical conclusion of this trend would be to change the female figures of the Bible such as Mary, the Mother of Jesus and Mary Magdalene to a gender neuter reference. If the female figures are not changed, it is not intellectually honest to change the gender of Jesus.

The drastic chopping of lyrics in the hymnals and the gender-neutral approach to the scripture texts of the Bible is a trend. What is next? Shall we change every text in scripture and song with which a few disagree? Shall all the personalities of religious history become nameless faces in an edited and diluted history? The logic of dropping the song from the hymnals rather that making the politically correct changes, would be to deny the facts of history. The language of the past centuries still speaks a language that many understand and appreciate. Is it wise to sacrifice the comfort and spiritual benefits of religious roots for current politics?   Shall the church abandon the glue that binds some to the fellowship for the sake of those who have already abandoned the church or have never embraced the message or cause of Christianity?

Christians should be sensitive to other people.   The effort, however, of some to use political correctness as an excuse for changing words in the old hymns of the church is an effort to impose a particular agenda on Christianity. Could one deny the feminine gender of Mary, the Mother of Jesus? In one new hymnal, the sex of baby Jesus is not mentioned. Faith of Our Fathers is now Faith of the Martyrs. Not altogether bad, but does it deny the contribution of ordinary men to the religious tradition? Did only the martyrs make a contribution to Christian heritage? Even the "right hand of God" is changed to the "mighty" or "strong" hand of God lest left-handed people be offended; could this be a consequence of the time when misguided educators were forcing all children to be right-handed?

The effort at more accurate translations of songs originating from the Latin may be both intellectually honest and needed. The Latin term *ex parents,* has been added to recognize parents rather than fathers.   Such moves demonstrate respect for one's forebears, both male and female and are in keeping with the gender-inclusive nature of scripture. In many cases, the effort to be politically correct has pushed the hymnal lyrics to the absurd.

Changing a few words without changing the heart and soul of individuals can never bring about desired change in the church. Such change can only come with a redirection of the internal nature of the human soul, and this is done within the social context of the individual.   Then, and only then, will a true change of heart make any change of words meaningful?

Heritage is a powerful force. It includes words, music, food, clothing, language, religious expressions and even racial and ethnic traditions. Heritage is a clear way to propagate the gospel to the next generation. Concern for the impact of social integration on the black church produced research to understand the consequences of integration on black church participation. It was discovered that the only factor that influenced individuals to attend a black church was the level of Black Heritage. One may be totally integrated in housing, education, and the work place, and desire to participate in the worship of a black church because of a high Black Heritage Index.   It is a logical assumption to generalize this fact to other cultures and ethnic groups. To ignore heritage is to limit the outreach of the church to the next generation. When the church deliberately fails to respect the heritage of a community or people, the process alienates the older folk and most certainly the present generation from participating in the church.

Music is a central part of culture and often a cornerstone of heritage. Standard hymns from the past and common tunes from early church memories often join to bind individuals to a particular church.   When one alters the words and meanings of a song, it is similar to messing with grandmother's receipt for Thanksgiving or Christmas dinner.   Food and music are central expressions of culture and an integral part of ones traditional heritage. The church should be building upon cultural and historical foundations of community heritage, rather than attempting to import changes that alienate individuals and families from worship.

My paternal grandmother had a unique receipt for "sugar cookies." These cookies were made for special occasions which reinforced their value to the family. Regretfully, the specific ingredients that my grandmother used are not available in the forms used by her. Her pinch of this and cup of that must have been different. The baking pan, the wood stove, and the secret pinch of "love" seem to be missing. The present cookies, although enjoyable, just do not taste the same. Perhaps there is a lesson for the church in the sugar cookie. Change the recipe, use a different stove, and when the ingredients have been processed, the outcome will be different. It may be impossible to reproduce the past, but it must be respected.

Heritage is part of the "love" mixture that makes the present society livable, but it will never be the same. Since change is inevitable, the church in each generation must deal with principles and heritage from the past, together with the essential substance of Christianity to effect individual and social change. The most essential and vital parts must not be left out of the new cultural mix. It requires the inclusion of the essential and vital parts. There must be an internal redirection of the protestant spirit that brings unity and agreement into the community of the saints. This is the true heritage of the Christian church. Nothing less will make Christianity work in the pluralistic society of America.

Other Books by Hollis L. Green

These books and Children's books written by Dr. Green
may be ordered through the website
GlobalEdAdvance.org

[ ] Why Churches Die
[ ] Sympathetic Leadership Cybernetics
[ ] Why Christianity Fails in America
[ ] SO TALES - Volume One
[ ] Philosophy of Adult Education
[ ] SO TALES Volume Two
[ ] DISCIPLESHIP
[ ] Why Wait Till Sunday?
[ ] Integrating Moral Values
[ ] Understanding Scientific Research
[ ] Interpreting an Author's Words
[ ] Titanic Lessons
[ ] A Composite New Testament Man
[ ] Things Learned and Passed to my Sons
[ ] Fighting the Amalekites
[ ] Love's Conversation
[ ] SO TALES Volume Three
[ ] Understanding Graduate Research
[ ] Lessons from Luke – NT 101
[ ] All Believers are Created Equal
[ ] Growing a New Testament Church
[ ] How to Build a Better Spouse Trap
[ ] Where in the World are you Going?
[ ] Hitching your Star to a Wagon
[ ] Climbing the Heights
[ ] SLEEPY TOWN Lullaby and Story

Order from:

GlobalEdAdvancePress
345 Barton Road at Lone Mountain, Dayton, TN 37321-7635 USA
GlobalEdAdvance@aol.com

GlobalEdAdvancePress
37321-7635 USA
ISBN 978-0-9796019-1-0

www.ingramcontent.com/pod-product-compliance
Lightning Source LLC
Chambersburg PA
CBHW061253110426
42742CB00012BA/1903